SYSTEMS THINKING:

"From Complexity... to Simplicity"

LEADING
STRATEGIC
CHANGE

The Systems Thinking Approach™
to
Business Excellence & Superior Results

"A Totally Integrated Systems Solution™"

Smart Start™:
An
Executive Briefing
on
Enterprise-Wide Change Management

by
Stephen G. Haines

President and Founder, the Centre for Strategic Management®

(6)

1420 Monitor Road • San Diego • California • 92110-1545 • (619) 275-6528 • Fax (619) 275-0324

One of the Centre's
"Enterprise-Wide Change Series"

Insanity ...
is doing the same things

in the same way

and

expecting different results.

— *Albert Einstein*

CHANGE is the only
constant in Life.

Note on Trademarks

The following Trademarks (™) are licensed to Systems Thinking Press and the Centre for Strategic Management® and may not be used without permission. All Trademarks must carry this mark (™) and be attributed to the Centre for Strategic Management® as follows:
• _____™ is a Registered Trademark of the Centre for Strategic Management (www.csmintl.com).

- Achieving Leadership Excellence™
- Business Excellence Architecture™
- Creating the People Edge™
- Enterprise-Wide Change™
- Quadruple Bottom Line™
- Reinventing Strategic Planning™

- Rollercoaster of Change™
- Smart Start™
- Strategic IQ™
- The ABCs of Strategic Management™
- The Simplicity of Systems Thinking™
- The Systems Thinking Approach™

- A Totally Integrated Systems Solution™

ebewc-cover.pmd

1420 Monitor Road • San Diego • California • 92110-1545 • (619) 275-6528 • Fax (619) 275-0324

**Changing Behaviors Always
Requires Deep Feelings**

—John Haaland

Thoughts vs. Actions

Thinking is easy. Acting is difficult.
To put one's thoughts into action
is the most difficult thing in the world.

—Goethe

The Centre's "Nothing to Lose" Guarantee

How to Get Started on Your Strategic Change Project:
A "Value-Added" One Day Meeting

Dear Participant:

As a way to get started on your Enterprise-Wide Change Process, we usually recommend a two-day Executive Briefing and Smart Start session with the Centre for Strategic Management®. In this session we are able to educate each other on any large scale change project you are planning to implement. It also allows us to get on the same page of music as to your situation. We will also mutually analyze, decide, and tailor what type of Enterprise-Wide Change management project, if any, should go beyond this event.

We are so confident of our ability to help you in this session that we offer a **"Nothing to Lose"** Guarantee for this event with your top management team. If you do not get "Value-Added" from the time we spend together, pay us our expenses only and the fee is waived.

In addition, there is **"No Further Obligation"** beyond the session. Both parties must agree that there is mutual benefit to proceed further.

As a pre-work to this Booklet and Smart Start process, we highly recommend you first read our 4-page Executive Summary Article on Enterprise-Wide Change. This booklet contains the handouts and overheads we use in this session. Without the article, this booklet will not be as useful and user friendly to you. If you need a copy of this article, please call us at the Centre.

Happy Reading,

Stephen G. Haines

Stephen G. Haines, President and Founder

Centre for Strategic Management
San Diego, California
(619) 275-6528

ebewc-cover.pmd

EXECUTIVE BRIEFING

LEADING ENTERPRISE-WIDE CHANGE™

OVERALL SMART START™ PURPOSES:

- To ensure successful execution of a Strategic Plan or a desired Enterprise-Wide Change and Transformation.

- To educate, assess, tailor, and organize an Enterprise-Wide Change Game Plan to your specific needs.

SPECIFIC OBJECTIVES

This workshop demonstrates how to:

1. Understand The Systems Thinking Approach™ and model for Business Excellence and Superior Results—the ABCs of Enterprise-Wide Change.

2. Build an Enterprise-Wide Change Game Plan to achieve and sustain a unique marketplace positioning and or ideal future vision.

3. Discover and appreciate the importance of the three elements present in all human interactions and dynamics of change—and why complex changes so often fail (the Iceberg Theory of Change).

4. Analyze and apply a menu of key structures as the leverage for enterprise-wide change management to your own organization and situation in order to design, build, and sustain the momentum of change.

5. Review the four key roles of the "Players of Change", and especially the key role of a Program Management Office.

6. Apply The Rollercoaster of Change™ and its many practical applications to any Organization Development intervention and change situation...as part of a totally integrated systems solution to Enterprise-Wide Change.

7. Assess your organization vs. the Five Organizational Capacity Elements needed to create and sustain an Enterprise-Wide Change Journey.

1420 Monitor Road • San Diego • California • 92110-1545 • (619) 275-6528 • Fax (619) 275-0324

One-Day Executive Briefing
Leading and Mastering Strategic Change
Agenda

I. Educate—Executive Briefing

9:00   1. **Welcome**, Purposes, Logistics, Introductions, Wants, Agenda

2. **Overview**
   - Overview of CSM—Strategic Management: Our Only Business
   - Questionnaire—change

3. **Three Types of Change**
   - Reactive/Strategic

4. *Essence of Strategic Management*
   - Real Formula = Change/Steps
   - Level of Excellence—Why Leaders Resist
   - Exercise—Why Change Fails

5. **Iceberg Theory of Change**

6. **Rollercoaster – Process**
   - Exercise — Death of a Loved One
   - Process Rollercoaster—then some of the 18 examples
   - Exercise — Principles of Change
   - Exercise — Unfreeze, etc. Which ones do you need?

12:00   **Lunch**

II. Organize and Tailor (Plan-to-Implement Tasks)

7. **Structures**
   - Exercise 11 structures — Which do you need?
   - Strategic Change Leadership Steering Committee & other structures
   - Leadership Skills

8. **Steps 7-10 of Strategic Planning Model**
   - Annual Planning/Budgeting – Appraisals – Plan-to-Implement, etc.

9. **Content**
   - A-B-C-D Systems Thinking
   - Exercise — Organizations as Living Systems Model
   - Impact Exercise
   - Menu Overall/Attunement/Alignment

10. **Summary — Putting It All Together**
   - Tailored to Your Needs
   - Resource Allocation
   - Yearly Map
   - Change Prototype
   - How do Get Started
   - Bottom Line Quote

4:00   **Close**

ebewc-cover.pmd

1420 Monitor Road • San Diego • California • 92110-1545 • (619) 275-6528 • Fax (619) 275-0324

ENTERPRISE-WIDE CHANGE™

A Smart Start™ to Enterprise-Wide Change

Table of Contents

SECTIONS

The Search for the Silver Bullet

Attempts to change organizations with the latest silver bullet ignored two powerful principles of organization:

#1   **Organizations are perfectly designed for the results they get.**

#2   Success comes from individuals who take accountability for their actions.

---

ebewc-cover.pmd

1420 Monitor Road • San Diego • California • 92110-1545 • (619) 275-6528 • Fax (619) 275-0324

Who Is The Centre?

STRATEGIC MANAGEMENT
"Our Only Business"

"Positioning Organizations to Create Customer Value"

❶ Strategic Edge

Creation of a Strategic Management System:
- **#2** Strategic Planning/Positioning
  - Business Planning
- **#3** Enterprise-Wide Change Management

"STRATEGIC BUSINESS DESIGN"

❷ People Edge

Attunement With People:
- **#4** Strategic HR Management
  - Executive Coaching and Team Building
- **#5** Leadership and Managament Development System

❸ Customer Edge

Alignment of Delivery:
- **#6** Strategic Marketing, Sales and Service
- **#7** Performance Excellence
  - Value Chain Management
  - Process Improvement

Greater Choice

Faster Response

#8 Customer Value

Better Service

Lower Cost

Higher Quality

#1 Our Foundation – Culture

❹ The Innovation & Systems Thinking ApproachSM

Systems Thinking • Innovation
• Our Core Values •
• Adult Learning • Fact-Based Decision-Making • Group Facilitation •

ebewc-cover.pmd

1420 Monitor Road • San Diego • California • 92110-1545 • (619) 275-6528 • Fax (619) 275-0324

EXAMPLES OF
ENTERPRISE-WIDE CHANGE™

Specific examples of Enterprise-Wide Change initiatives and activities include:

- Installing an Enterprise Resource Planning system (ERP)
- Creating a new culture
- Focusing on business and operational excellence initiatives
- Conducting mergers, acquisitions, joint ventures and alliances
- Installing major new technologies
- Executing strategic and business planning
- Becoming more customer-focused
- Becoming a global company
- Improving customer service
- Desiring major growth and a leap in expansion
- Downsizing, outsourcing, and major cutbacks
- Restructuring and redesigning the organization
- Improving Six-Sigma and quality
- Improving the supply chain management
- Developing and deploying major new products
- Transformation of an entire enterprise
- Significantly increasing creativity and innovation
- Creating new businesses

Enterprise-Wide Change includes many of the traditional change interventions in which OD consultants are typically involved, such as team-building, visioning, leadership and executive succession, talent development, HR planning, and change execution.

ebewc-cover.pmd

1420 Monitor Road • San Diego • California • 92110-1545 • (619) 275-6528 • Fax (619) 275-0324

THE UNIQUENESS OF ENTERPRISE-WIDE CHANGE™

Unlike traditional change efforts, Enterprise-Wide Change through a Systems Thinking Approach is a complex, systemic, laborious undertaking. It is not to be taken lightly.

It is fundamentally different from other traditional change processes.

A doctor would be guilty of malpractice if he or she operated on a patient without appropriate knowledge, skills, and a deep understanding of anatomy, genetics, the patient's current health, and medical history.

Likewise, leaders and change consultants cannot responsibly impose change initiatives on their own "patients" (the organization as a whole, fellow managers, employees, customers, suppliers, owners, the community) without a full understanding of EWC's unique demands.

The six distinct characteristics of EWC that separate it from less comprehensive change initiatives are:

1. *Major structural/fundamental impact*—EWC has a major structural and fundamental impact on the entire organization or business unit in which change is to occur.

2. *Strategic in scope*—The change to be effected is strategic in nature. It links to the business's unique positioning in the marketplace (even the public sector marketplace).

3. *Complex, chaotic, and/or radical*—The change is complex and chaotic in nature, or will constitute a radical departure from the current state. (Even to the point that desired outcomes and approaches to achieve them may be unclear).

4. *Large-scale and transformational*—The scale of desired change is large and will result in a significantly different enterprise.

5. *Long timeframe*—The desired change will require years, with multiple phases and stages of major changes.

6. *Cultural change*—The rules of the game change; the norms, guideposts, values, and guides to behavior.

1420 Monitor Road • San Diego • California • 92110-1545 • (619) 275-6528 • Fax (619) 275-0324

TYPES OF CHANGE MANAGEMENT

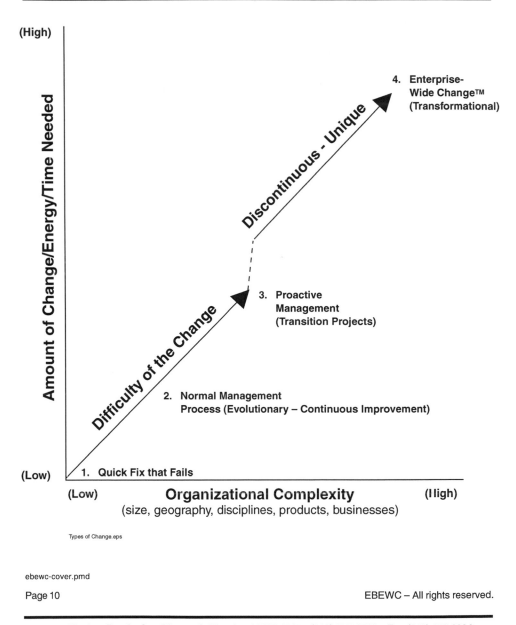

Types of Change.eps

1420 Monitor Road • San Diego • California • 92110-1545 • (619) 275-6528 • Fax (619) 275-0324

ENTERPRISE-WIDE CHANGE TYPES

	Incremental	**Enterprise-Wide**
Proactive	3. **Transitional** Management (Projects)	4. **Strategic** (Transformational & Cultural)
Reactive	1. **Quick Fix** (That fails)	2. **Fine Tuning** (Evolutionary & Continuous Improvement)

ebewc-cover.pmd

1420 Monitor Road • San Diego • California • 92110-1545 • (619) 275-6528 • Fax (619) 275-0324

STANDARD "KNEE-JERK" SIMPLISTIC IMPLEMENTATION TECHNIQUES

(QUICK FIXES THAT FAIL)

Question: Which do you do? Check the #.

1. _____ Form a team or committee; hold a meeting.
2. _____ Set up a suggestion/recognition system.
3. _____ Set up a training program(s).
4. _____ Improve communications—videos, policy, newsletter, memos.
5. _____ Define a Vision, Mission, and Values.
6. _____ Improve our performance appraisal form.
7. _____ Empower people.
8. _____ Hire a staff expert/delegate it (i.e., HR, QC, T/D, MIS, Planning)
9. _____ Hold a yearly retreat.
10. _____ Problem solve it: one issue at a time.
11. _____ Cut costs across the board.
12. _____ Have a hiring freeze.
13. _____ Hold someone accountable; punish or terminate him or her.
14. _____ Set up a merit increase; "pay-for-performance" program.
15. _____ Have a flurry of activity (but short-lived)

_____ Total Points

What Else?

16. _____
17. _____
18. _____
19. _____
20. _____

ebewc-cover.pmd

1420 Monitor Road • San Diego • California • 92110-1545 • (619) 275-6528 • Fax (619) 275-0324

SMART START™

Major change efforts fail to achieve their intended results 75-80% of the time

Two Goals:
- Serve your clients today
- Build for the future (Enterprise-Wide Change Management)

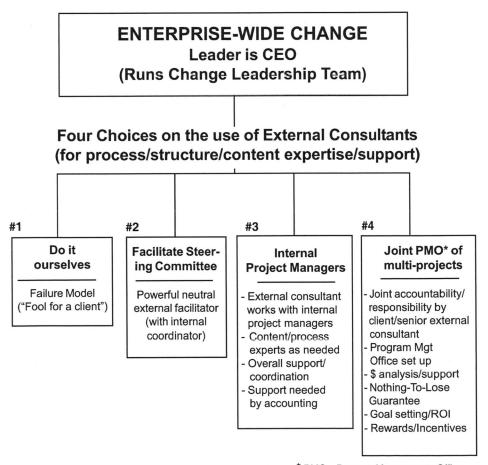

ENTERPRISE-WIDE CHANGE
Leader is CEO
(Runs Change Leadership Team)

**Four Choices on the use of External Consultants
(for process/structure/content expertise/support)**

#1
Do it ourselves

Failure Model
("Fool for a client")

#2
Facilitate Steering Committee

Powerful neutral external facilitator (with internal coordinator)

#3
Internal Project Managers

- External consultant works with internal project managers
- Content/process experts as needed
- Overall support/ coordination
- Support needed by accounting

#4
Joint PMO* of multi-projects

- Joint accountability/ responsibility by client/senior external consultant
- Program Mgt Office set up
- $ analysis/support
- Nothing-To-Lose Guarantee
- Goal setting/ROI
- Rewards/Incentives

* PMO = Program Management Office

ebewc-cover.pmd

1420 Monitor Road • San Diego • California • 92110-1545 • (619) 275-6528 • Fax (619) 275-0324

SMART START™ : A TWO-DAY SESSION

(EDUCATE—ASSESS—TAILOR—ORGANIZE)

I. **Educate**
1. Iceberg Theory of Change (content – process – structure)
2. Rollercoaster of Change
3. Menu of Structures for Change
4. 3 Goals, 3 Premises, ABCs Model
5. System of Innovation
6. Why Change Fails?

II. **Assess**
1. Summary of Desired Major Changes (from the Strategic Plan)
2. Strategic Plan/Annual Plan completion
3. Year #1 Strategic Change Process
4. Leadership Development Assessment/System
5. Multi-year Cultural Change Effort (Executive Development)
6. "Business Excellence Architecture" and "Building on the Baldrige" Assessment
7. Innovation Audit

III. **Tailor**
1. Yearly Comprehensive Map of Implementation (single page Game Plan)
2. Change Leadership Team (#1 Absolute) – regular meetings – how often
3. PMO Operation
4. Performance/Rewards Form/System to Reinforce the Change
5. Rollout/Communicate to Organization (including Trifold)
6. Strategic People Plan ("Creating the People Edge")
7. Implementing Transformational/Culture Change (violate the norms)
8. "One Agenda—One Day" meetings on key nuggets
9. *GoInnovate!* System of Innovation

IV. **Organize**
1. Change Leadership Team
2. Project Management Office (PMO)
3. Project Teams
4. Internal/External Coordination (Change Agent Cadre)
5. Employee Development Board
6. Key Success Measure Tracking – measuring
7. Personal Leadership Plans (PLPs)

ebewc-cover.pmd

1420 Monitor Road • San Diego • California • 92110-1545 • (619) 275-6528 • Fax (619) 275-0324

THE ABCs OF
STRATEGIC MANAGEMENT™
(Planning - People - Leadership - Change)

DEFINITION:

Strategic Planning

Plus

Strategic (Enterprise-Wide) Change

Plus

Leadership and Management

THREE GOALS:

Work On The Enterprise:
#1   Design Clarity of Purpose
     (Strategic, Business, and Annual Plans)

Work In The Enterprise:
#2   Build Simplicity of Execution
     (Successful Implementation and Enterprise-Wide Change)

Check On The Enterprise:
#3   Sustain a System of Results
     (Annual Strategic Review and Update)

The Results:
     Business Excellence and Superior Results
     (Year After Year)

THREE MAIN PREMISES:

#1   Planning and Change are *the Primary* job of Leadership

#2   "People Support What They Help Create"

#3   Use Systems Thinking
     Focus on Outcomes – Serve the Customer

Five Phases of STRATEGIC MANAGEMENT

A Vision Values

B Measures Feedback

C Assessment Strategies

D Action Change

E Environment Scan

– Results –

Business Excellence and Superior Results
(Year After Year)

abcsm.ops

4th Edition • Adapted from General Systems Theory, and Haines Associates, our experiences, a "Best Practices" literature search, and client feedback.

© 2004 Revised • Centre for Strategic Management® • All rights reserved.
1420 Monitor Road, San Diego, CA 92110 • (619) 275-6528 • FAX (619) 275-0324
Website: www.csmintl.com • Email: info@csmintl.com

ebewc-cover.pmd

LEVERAGE POINTS FOR CHANGE (EWC)

Best Practices Report
International Quality Study (IQS)

**American Quality Foundation
and Ernst & Young**

Summary of Study
- extensive statistical study
- 945 management practices over 580 organizations (84% response rate)
- in U.S., Japan, Canada, Germany
- automotive, banking, computer, health care industries

Best Practices Lead to High Performance (defined as:)
1. Market performance (perceived quality index)
2. Operations (productivity) performance (value-added per employee)
3. Financial performance (ROA)

Only Three Universally Beneficial Practices
- Only three (3) universally beneficial practices with a significant impact on performance regardless of starting position (rest is a "fit" question of organization – environment – performance)
    1. Strategic Planning/Deployment (Implementation/Innovation)
    2. Business Process improvement methods
    3. Continuous broadening of your range (and depth) of management practices (to make additional gains in performance)

Background
- Fundamental organizational activities — managing people, processes, technology, and strategy

ebewc-cover.pmd

1420 Monitor Road • San Diego • California • 92110-1545 • (619) 275-6528 • Fax (619) 275-0324

CRITICAL ISSUES LIST

What are the 5-10 most important critical/strategic issues facing you today as an organization?

1.

2.

3.

4.

5.

6.

7.

8.

9.

10.

If Strategic Planning is going smoothly, we're doing something wrong

(unless we have infinite resources).

Challenge the Obvious!

Note: Use this list as the content framework and "grounding" for the strategic thinking process. Bring it out at the end of the planning process to ensure you've covered these issues adequately.

ebewc-cover.pmd

1420 Monitor Road • San Diego • California • 92110-1545 • (619) 275-6528 • Fax (619) 275-0324

WANTS LIST – YOUR LEARNINGS

By the time you walk out the door at the end of this session, what are the 2-6 key questions, topics, and other concepts you WANT covered?

1.

2.

3.

4.

5.

6.

A LIFETIME OF PROSPERITY

> - If you want to be prosperous for a year, grow grain.
> - If you want to be prosperous for ten years, grow trees.
> - If you want to be prosperous for a lifetime, grow people.
>
> Proverb

ebewc-cover.pmd

1420 Monitor Road • San Diego • California • 92110-1545 • (619) 275-6528 • Fax (619) 275-0324

SECTION I
OVERVIEW OF
ENTERPRISE-WIDE CHANGE
"WHY IT FAILS"

75% of All Major Change Efforts Fail!

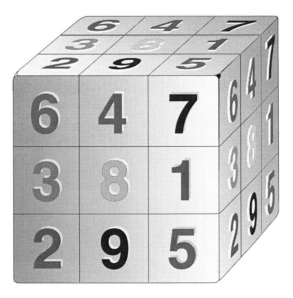

Why?
Rubik's Cubes and Organizations
are Both Complex Systems

ebewc01.pmd

1420 Monitor Road • San Diego • California • 92110-1545 • (619) 275-6528 • Fax (619) 275-0324

HIGH FAILURE RATES

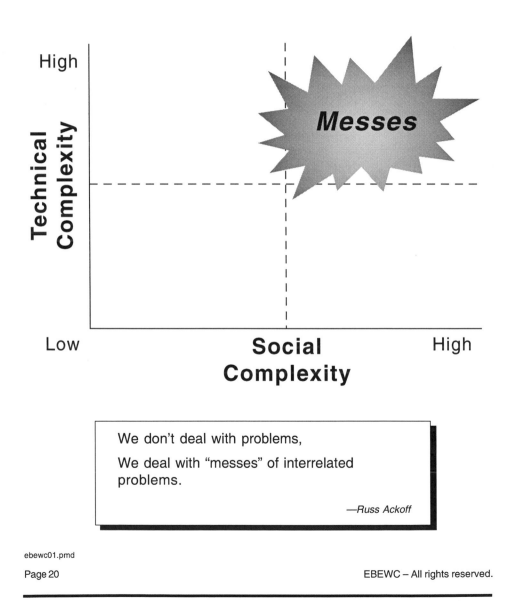

We don't deal with problems,

We deal with "messes" of interrelated problems.

—*Russ Ackoff*

1420 Monitor Road • San Diego • California • 92110-1545 • (619) 275-6528 • Fax (619) 275-0324

INITIATING CHANGES – MACHIAVELLI

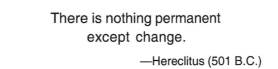

There is nothing permanent
except change.

—Hereclitus (501 B.C.)

"It should be borne in mind that there is nothing more difficult to arrange, more doubtful of success, and more dangerous to carry through than initiating changes in a state's constitution.

The innovator makes enemies of all those who prospered under the older order, and only lukewarm support is forthcoming from those who would prosper under the new. Their support is lukewarm partly from fear of their adversaries, who have the existing laws on their side, and partly because men are generally incredulous, never really trusting new things unless they have tested them by experience.

In consequence, whenever those who oppose the changes can do so, they attack vigorously, and the defense made by the others is only lukewarm.

So both the innovator and his friends are endangered together."

—Machiavelli

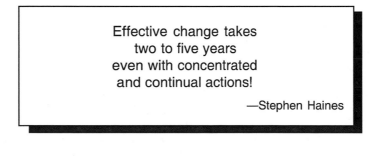

Effective change takes
two to five years
even with concentrated
and continual actions!

—Stephen Haines

ebewc01.pmd

1420 Monitor Road • San Diego • California • 92110-1545 • (619) 275-6528 • Fax (619) 275-0324

THE DESTRUCTIVE CHANGE MYTH

"Salute and Execute"

Everyone

- is for it;
- feels they understand it;
- thinks execution is only a matter of following natural inclinations;
- feels that problems are caused by other people.

Instant Pudding
vs. Leading and Encouraging

Many times managers read long-range plans, nod in agreement, and then wait for something to begin. For instance, when companies begin their quality improvement process, which is a complete strategy of changing the management culture, many folks will be concerned early that nothing is happening. They expect the process to do it all by itself.

They think that educating people, forming teams, and having meetings starts some sort of mystic plasma flowing. They don't realize immediately that management has to lead, and in some cases drag, people along.

Constant encouragement has to be given and consistent enthusiasm displayed.

BIG THREE ENTERPRISE-WIDE FAILURE ISSUES:

How to Fail to Achieve Your Intended Results:

"Guarantee of Failure Up Front":

Yes/No?

_____ **#1. Analytic and Piecemeal Approaches to a System's Problem**

- Involving multiple mindsets, frameworks, consultants and fads/silver bullets
- Instead of a *Systems Thinking Approach* and insisting on *Watertight Integrity*

_____ **#2. Mainly Focusing on an Economic Alignment of Delivery**

- Involving a primary focus on productivity, processes, and bottom-line efficiencies
- Instead of combining this with "attunement" issues below

_____ **#3. Mainly Focusing on Cultural Attunement and Involvement with People**

- Involving a primary focus on egalitarian, participative, democratic, people processes
- Instead of combining this approach and #2 above (economic alignment)

Are any of these an issue in your organization? Write " Yes " or "No" above

VERSUS:

"A Totally Integrated Systems Solution":

- An *Enterprise-Wide Systems Thinking Approach*™ to **Business Excellence** – with a *Quadruple Bottom Line* measurement system (economics–employees–customers–society)
- *That dramatically increases* **Superior Results***:* (Profits–Growth–Culture–Sustainability)

ebewc01.pmd

1420 Monitor Road • San Diego • California • 92110-1545 • (619) 275-6528 • Fax (619) 275-0324

Why Some Business Leaders Resist Change

Have a lot to protect - a vested interest in the status quo	82%
Don't like to lose control of events	79%
Don't know what to do about change	77%
Too short-term oriented	76%
Don't get rewarded for change	42%

These are a few key findings of a landmark survey of Fortune 1,000 executives, conducted in the U.S. by the Gallup Organization of Princeton, NJ.

Proudfoot Change Management, *Forward Thinking,* Spring 1994

ebewc01.pmd

1420 Monitor Road • San Diego • California • 92110-1545 • (619) 275-6528 • Fax (619) 275-0324

LEVELS OF EXCELLENCE

> *The pursuit of mediocrity*
> *is*
> *always successful.*

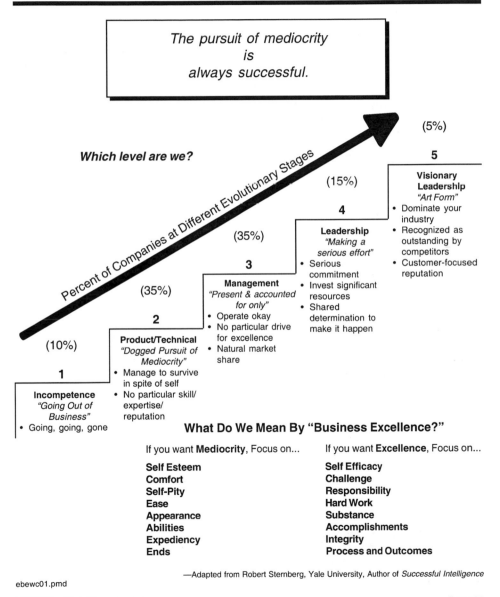

Which level are we?

Percent of Companies at Different Evolutionary Stages

(5%)

5

Visionary Leadership
"Art Form"
- Dominate your industry
- Recognized as outstanding by competitors
- Customer-focused reputation

(15%)

4

Leadership
"Making a serious effort"
- Serious commitment
- Invest significant resources
- Shared determination to make it happen

(35%)

3

Management
"Present & accounted for only"
- Operate okay
- No particular drive for excellence
- Natural market share

(35%)

2

Product/Technical
"Dogged Pursuit of Mediocrity"
- Manage to survive in spite of self
- No particular skill/ expertise/ reputation

(10%)

1

Incompetence
"Going Out of Business"
- Going, going, gone

What Do We Mean By "Business Excellence?"

If you want **Mediocrity**, Focus on...	If you want **Excellence**, Focus on...
Self Esteem	**Self Efficacy**
Comfort	**Challenge**
Self-Pity	**Responsibility**
Ease	**Hard Work**
Appearance	**Substance**
Abilities	**Accomplishments**
Expediency	**Integrity**
Ends	**Process and Outcomes**

—Adapted from Robert Sternberg, Yale University, Author of *Successful Intelligence*

ebewc01.pmd

1420 Monitor Road • San Diego • California • 92110-1545 • (619) 275-6528 • Fax (619) 275-0324

WHY CHANGE EFFORTS USUALLY FAIL

"Most companies don't fail for lack of talent or strategic vision. **They fail for lack of execution**—the routine **"blocking and tackling"** that great companies consistently do well and always strive to do better."

—T.J. Rodgers, *No-Excuses Management*

1. **Underestimate Systems Complexity.** Top level executives tend to underestimate what it will take. They have unrealistic expectations and fail to understand that the organization is a system of interdependent parts and different levels (individual, team, organization). Thus, knee-jerk simple and direct cause and effect solutions dealing with symptoms only is the result. Use of simple solutions versus appreciated the complexities of interdependent organizations as systems doesn't work.

2. **Details Lacking.** The failure to specify in sufficient detail the actual work required to implement the change; especially in larger organizations (content/process/structure).

3. **Change Knowledge Missing.** The failure to know, follow and use the "Rollercoaster of Change" as to how people go through change psychologically. That change has three dimensions—cultural, political, and rational. Discounting the cost of the psychological effects of change or investing in human assets.

4. **Reinforcers Lacking.** The lack of realignment of the business control systems such as performance measures, budgets, MIS, compensation, values. Absence of support and reinforcement/rewards for the new changes.

5. **Accountability Failure.** The lack of specific accountability, responsibility and consequences at every level of the organization. Inadequate executive accountability and leadership of the change—failure to know their role is the active "champions" of the changes.

6. **Time Pressure.** Too many changes at once and a quick-fix mentality. Too short-term an orientation by the senior executives. Even greed, obsession with short-term, fast buck, and super profits. Failure to budget adequate "lead" or "lag" time.

7. **Management Resistance.** Middle and first line management resistance, apathy, or abdication.

8. **Turf Battles.** Opposing and conflicting messages and turf battles in and from top management along with a split of executive views (as cancer) towards the change. Lack of focused and clear direction, teamwork, and consistency.

9. **Change Structures Missing.** Missing the formal structures, processes, and needed dedicated resources to lead and follow-up on the desired changes.

ebewc01.pmd

continued

1420 Monitor Road • San Diego • California • 92110-1545 • (619) 275-6528 • Fax (619) 275-0324

WHY CHANGE EFFORTS USUALLY FAIL

10. **Reactive Posture.** The failure to act in advance in a proactive fashion; allowing issues to fester and grow, or reacting in a eclectic fashion without a plan or organized framework and philosophy.

11. **Status Quo.** Vested interests and power in the status quo, the auto pilot mindset/ complacency and the hierarchy can defeat most change efforts.

12. **Stubbornness.** Stupidity and stubbornness by senior management in not using proven research on what works. Instead, relying on their own inadequate models of change, mindless imitation of the latest fad, or using outmoded theories of motivation.

13. **Control Issues.** Senior executive desire to maintain control over people and events (vs. strategic consistency and operational flexibility) and their low tolerance for uncertainty and ambiguity.

14. **Participative Management Skills Lacking.** Inadequate senior management knowledge and skills on what to do and how to manage change; just plain poor execution—the routine blocking and tackling that great organizations do consistently well. Lack of skills by managers and executives in "participative management" techniques; including those of trainer, coach, and facilitator. This is where an organization's greatest assets are; with management—so they will empower and utilize employees as their other greatest assets.

15. **Fatal Assumption Made.** Making the fatal assumption that "everyone is for it, understands it, and that execution is only a matter of following your natural inclinations.

16. **Redistribution Failure.** Failure to redistribute financial resources based on future priorities/ direction through lack of strategic budgeting. Denial and unwillingness to make the required "tough decisions."

17. **Politically Correct Desire.** The perception that it isn't politically correct to be a strong leader with convictions, expertise, and strong directions/opinions. Putting up with poor performance. This used to be the opposite; namely that megalomania—one man show is what works—the benevolent or not-too-benevolent dictator.

18. **Initial Bias Wrong.** A bias towards thinking that initially communicating direction, educating people, forming teams, and holding meetings will result in success. Bureaucracy and trivial activities will fill up the time allotted.

19. **Lack of Senior Management Modeling.** The unwillingness of senior management to model and gain credibility and trust towards the desired changes first, and to change their leadership and management practices and communications.

ebewc01.pmd

continued

1420 Monitor Road • San Diego • California • 92110-1545 • (619) 275-6528 • Fax (619) 275-0324

WHY CHANGE EFFORTS USUALLY FAIL

20. **Multiple Consultants and Philosophies.** Ineffective use of multiple consultants and/or philosophies on a piecemeal basis. Paradigms and belief in analytic approaches to a systems problem.

21. **Lack of Customer-Focus.** Failure to focus on customer wants and needs and satisfaction as your only reason for existence.

22. **Skeptics Not Involved.** Failure to value skeptics and to enroll a critical mass for change. The lack of use of high involvement methods, the Parallel Process, and opportunities for personal and group growth and development. People support what they help create.

23. **Poor Cross-Functional Teamwork.** Lack of horizontal, cross-functional communications, teamwork, collaboration, and task forces.

24. **Unsupportive Organizational Design.** Unsupportive organizational structure and design to the desired changes.

25. **Lack of Follow-Through.** The failure to follow-through and sustain the energy, momentum, buy-in and stay-in, effort and commitment as well as accountability over the long-term. Perseverance in the face of the first difficulty (vs. pulling the plug) is the key.

26. **Middle Manager Skills Lacking.** Failure to direct, train, empower, leverage, support, and build the skills of middle managers and first line supervisors.

27. **Poor Communications of Direction.** Poor communications and lack of clarity/stump speech about the directions; the single most pressing problem in many organizations.

28. **Cherished Values Violated.** Violation of cherished values without clear understanding of why, and what replaces it.

29. **Debrief and Learn.** Failure to conduct postmortems, debriefs and distillation of learnings from previous change efforts.

30. **Cultural Diversity.** Failure to understand local, global, cultural or ethnic diversity—thus taking wrong, insensitive actions.

31. **Lack of a Game Plan.** Failure to have an "Implementation Game Plan" for the process of change—note just the content/tasks of the Strategic Plan.

32. **Political Environment.** The presence of a political and politicized environment and multiple agendas that block real progress.

33. **Powerlessness.** Inability to have decisions and change made in a timely manner (paralysis/bottlenecking)

ebewc01.pmd

1420 Monitor Road • San Diego • California • 92110-1545 • (619) 275-6528 • Fax (619) 275-0324

WHY CHANGE EFFORTS USUALLY FAIL — SUMMARY

1. Which 3-5 efforts are our change strengths? Why?

Strengths	Why?
1.	
2.	
3.	
4.	
5.	

2. Which 3+ mistakes do we usually make?

Mistakes	Why?	Implications?
1.		
2.		
3.		
4.		
5.		
6.		
7.		
8.		

ebewc01.pmd

1420 Monitor Road • San Diego • California • 92110-1545 • (619) 275-6528 • Fax (619) 275-0324

THE SECRET OF CONSTANT GROWTH*

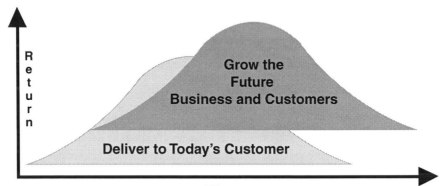

Return

Grow the
Future
Business and Customers

Deliver to Today's Customer

Servicing.eps

Time

If you always do
what you've always done
you'll always get
what you've always gotten.

The Difficulty of Enterprise-Wide Change Management

1. Managing the Day-to-Day Business/ Organization

2. Managing the Change Process

Under stress and a heavy load, which management activity above loses out?

---

*© Andrew Papageorge, GoInnovate! - www.GoInnovate.com

ebewc01.pmd

1420 Monitor Road • San Diego • California • 92110-1545 • (619) 275-6528 • Fax (619) 275-0324

SECTION II
THE SYSTEMS THINKING APPROACH™
TO
SUPERIOR RESULTS

Systems Thinking

is finding patterns and relationships,
and learning to reinforce
or change these patterns
to fulfill your vision and mission.

1420 Monitor Road • San Diego • California • 92110-1545 • (619) 275-6528 • Fax (619) 275-0324

Our Level of Thinking

Problems that are created
by our current level of thinking
can't be solved
by that same level of thinking.

—*Albert Einstein*

So . . . if we generally use
analytical thinking,
we now need
real "Systems Thinking"
to resolve our issues.

—*Stephen G. Haines*

1420 Monitor Road • San Diego • California • 92110-1545 • (619) 275-6528 • Fax (619) 275-0324

Why Thinking Matters

The way you think creates the results you get.

The most powerful way to impact the quality of your results is to improve the ways you think.

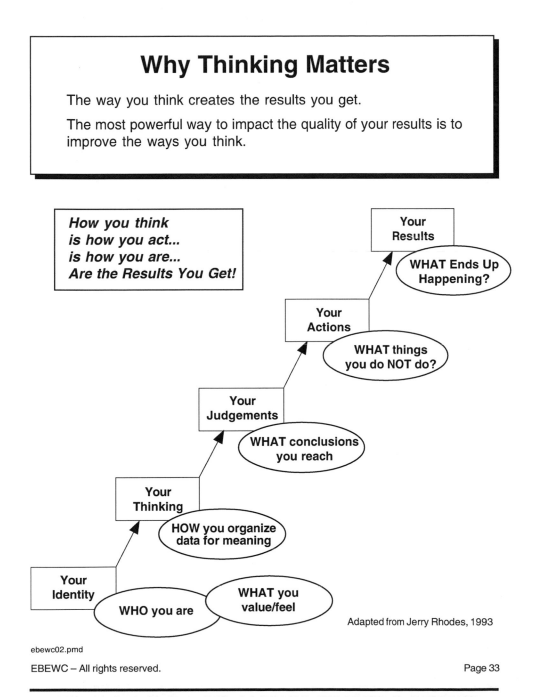

How you think
is how you act...
is how you are...
Are the Results You Get!

Your Results

WHAT Ends Up Happening?

Your Actions

WHAT things you do NOT do?

Your Judgements

WHAT conclusions you reach

Your Thinking

HOW you organize data for meaning

Your Identity

WHO you are

WHAT you value/feel

Adapted from Jerry Rhodes, 1993

ebewc02.pmd

1420 Monitor Road • San Diego • California • 92110-1545 • (619) 275-6528 • Fax (619) 275-0324

ORGANIZATIONS AS LIVING SYSTEMS (THE NATURAL ORDER OF LIFE)

How you think ... is how you act ... is how you are!

We need to learn:

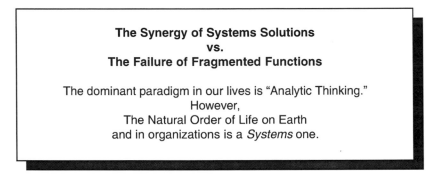

The Synergy of Systems Solutions
vs.
The Failure of Fragmented Functions

The dominant paradigm in our lives is "Analytic Thinking."
However,
The Natural Order of Life on Earth
and in organizations is a *Systems* one.

Thus, analytic approaches (and analytic thinking) to systems problems in everyday life and organizations is now *bankrupt!*

The good news is that this new "Systems Thinking Paradigm" is beginning to emerge; witness the use of new systems-oriented words, such as:

fit, integration, collaboration, cooperation, teamwork, partnerships,

alliances, linkages, stakeholders, holistic, seamless, boundaryless, system, etc.

Our Systems Model "bridges this gap" — opening up whole new vistas and THE newly emerging paradigm that more properly fits with reality . . . and the **Natural Order of the Universe and Life.**

Systems vs. Analytic Thinking

In *Systems Thinking*—the whole is primary and the parts are secondary.

vs.

In *Analytic Thinking*—the parts are primary and the whole is secondary.

ebewc02.pmd

1420 Monitor Road • San Diego • California • 92110-1545 • (619) 275-6528 • Fax (619) 275-0324

ANALYTICAL THINKING (AND SPECIALIZATION)

("Micro Right—Macro Wrong")

1. IRS Rules—over 4000 pages

2. Health Care—thousands of small specialized entities based on singular type grants

3. Social Services—thousands of small specialized entities based on singular categorical type grants

4. Specialized Government Districts—water districts, assessment districts, school districts, etc.

5. Separate Cities and Counties—little or no geographic separation

6. Federal Intelligence Agencies—16 of them

7. Congressional Subcommittees—too numerous to mention

8. California—7,700 page education code

9. U.S. Naval Academy regulations (from 10 to 1000+ pages in 150 years)

10. Sears—29,000 pages of policies and procedures

11. Federal Government Policies and Procedures—Al Gore's "Stacks and Stacks."

What else can you think of?

Does this kind of control really work? What are the alternatives?

> **Micro Smart or Macro Smart**
> **(Analytic or Systems Thinking)**
> "Are you micro smart
> and yet
> macro dumb?"

ebewc02.pmd

1420 Monitor Road • San Diego • California • 92110-1545 • (619) 275-6528 • Fax (619) 275-0324

ANALYTIC VS. SYSTEMS THINKING
(Strategic Consistency Yet Operational Flexibility)

(Outside – In – Outside Again: Both Are Then Useful)

○━ Success Key: *Organizational Systems Fit, Alignment, and Integrity*

Analytic Thinking (Analysis of Today)	vs.		Systems Thinking (Synthesis for the Future)
1. We/they	vs.	1.	Customers/stakeholders
2. Independent	vs.	2.	Interdependent
3. Activities/tasks/means	and	3.	Outcomes/ends
4. Problem solving	and	4.	Solution seeking
5. Today is fine	vs.	5.	Shared vision of future
6. Units/departments	and	6.	Total organization
7. Silo mentality	vs.	7.	Cross-functional teamwork
8. Closed environment	vs.	8.	Openness and feedback
9. Department goals	and	9.	Shared core strategies
10. Strategic Planning project	vs.	10.	Strategic Management System
11. Hierarchy and controls	and	11.	Serve the customer
12. Not my job	vs.	12.	Communications and collaboration
13. Isolated change	vs.	13.	Systemic change
14. Linear/begin-end	vs.	14.	Circular/repeat cycles
15. Little picture/view	vs.	15.	Big picture/holistic perspective
16. Short-term	and	16.	Long-term
17. Separate issues	vs.	17.	Related issues
18. Symptoms	and	18.	Root causes
19. Isolated Events	and	19.	Patterns/trends
20. Activities/Actions	and	20.	Clear outcome expectations (Goals/Values)
Sum: Parts are Primary	vs.		Whole is Primary

STOP Using "Analytic Approaches to Systems Problems"

Systems vs. Analytic Thinking

In Systems Thinking —the whole is primary and the parts are secondary
vs.
In Analytic Thinking—the parts are primary and the whole is secondary.

ebewc02.pmd

1420 Monitor Road • San Diego • California • 92110-1545 • (619) 275-6528 • Fax (619) 275-0324

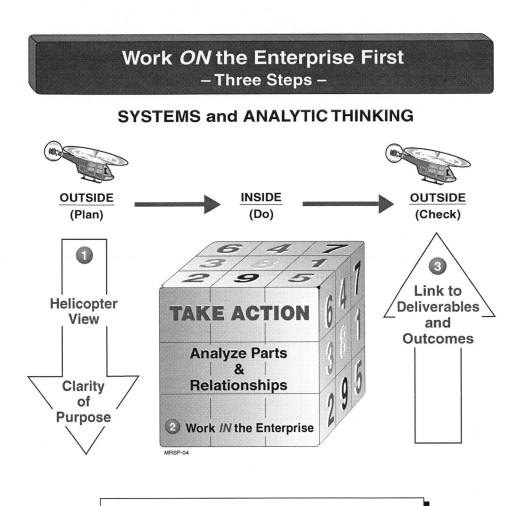

Work *ON* the Enterprise First
— Three Steps —

SYSTEMS and ANALYTIC THINKING

OUTSIDE
(Plan)

INSIDE
(Do)

OUTSIDE
(Check)

① Helicopter View

Clarity of Purpose

TAKE ACTION

Analyze Parts & Relationships

② Work *IN* the Enterprise

MRSP-04

③ Link to Deliverables and Outcomes

Backwards Thinking
"Life can only be understood backwards,
but must be lived forwards."

—*Soren Kierkegaard*
famous 19th century Danish philosopher

---

ebewc02.pmd

1420 Monitor Road • San Diego • California • 92110-1545 • (619) 275-6528 • Fax (619) 275-0324

THE SYSTEMS THINKING APPROACH™
"The Natural Way the World Works"

"A New Orientation to Life" – Our Core Technology
STRATEGIC THINKING
"From Complexity to Simplicity"

Systems: Systems are made up of a set of components that work together for the overall objective of the whole (output).

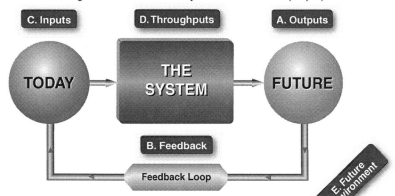

Backwards Thinking:
Five Strategic Thinking Questions – In Sequence:

A Where do we want to be? (i.e., our ends, outcomes, purposes, goals, holistic vision)

B How will we know when we get there? (i.e., the customers' needs and wants connected into a quantifiable feedback system)

C Where are we now? (i.e., today's issues and problems)

D How do we get there? (i.e., close the gap from C ➡ A in a complete, holistic way)

E Ongoing:
What will/may change in your environment in the future?

vs. Analytic Thinking Which:

1 Starts with today and the current state, issues, and problems

2 Breaks the issues and/or problems into their smallest components

3 Solves each component separately (i.e., maximizes the solution)

4 Has no far-reaching vision or goal (just the absence of a problem)

NOTE: In Systems Thinking, the whole is primary and the parts are secondary (not vice-versa).

"If you don't know where you're going, any road will get you there."

Why Thinking Matters

ebewc02.|

1420 Monitor Road • San Diego • California • 92110-1545 • (619) 275-6528 • Fax (619) 275-0324

STRATEGIC MANAGEMENT SYSTEM (SMS)

- Is Managed as a complete "Systems Change"
  (with strategic/annual/individual plans, budgets, and measurements)
- Is Successful if it is:
  1. Vision inspired and shared
  2. Mission/customer focused
  3. Values/culturally based
  4. Strategically driven
  5. Outcome/results oriented
- Its hallmark is:

  *Strategic Consistency **Yet** Operational Flexibility*

  "Focus – Focus – Focus"

Strategic Management System

"I need to stress at this point that an effective management system is more than just the sum of the parts . . . *it is a set of integrated policies, practices, and behaviors.*

Sometimes having a good management system is confused with having high-quality employees. This is a mistake—the two are quite different in some important ways: having high quality employees does not assure an organization of having a sustainable competitive advantage or even a short-term advantage."

—Edward J. Lawler, III
The Ultimate Advantage:
Creating the High-Involvement Organization

---

ebewc02.pmd

1420 Monitor Road • San Diego • California • 92110-1545 • (619) 275-6528 • Fax (619) 275-0324

"TOP 10" CLUES TO ANALYTIC THINKING

You know you are in the presence of *analytic thinking* when:

1. A lack of *clear purposes or outcomes is missing* from the discussions

2. People are asking or debating *"artificial either/or"* questions

3. Discussions are about the *"one best way"* to do something without asking those closest to the issue for their solutions ("People Support What They Help Create")

4. Discussions are focused on a direct *"cause and effect"* without considering circular causality or environmental factors

5. *Simplistic Knee-Jerk Solutions and Quick Fixes* are being suggested without digging for the multiple root causes

6. Issues and projects are being separated into silo discussions instead of *looking for the relatedness, the impact and the integration* of them with other parts of the organization

7. Discussions are activity-oriented without *Clarity of Purpose*

8. An *early project activity is an assessment* of the situation (SWOT?) instead of first starting with a Future Environmental Scan and Desired Outcomes

9. Decisions are being made without first exploring their *Unintended Consequences*

10. *Feedback and openness are being sacrificed* in the name of politeness and fragile egos ("Skeptics Are My Best Friends")

11. The complexity of the discussions, terminology and proposed solutions are such that they will die of their own weight (Simplicity Wins the Game Every Time)

Simplicity and Systems Thinking Wins The Game Every Time!

In Summary:
- We are governed by the natural laws of life and living as open/living systems on earth.
  —so—
- **A successful participant must learn the rules**

- **Analytical thinking is old Industrial Revolution thinking.**

---

ebewc02.pmd

MANY POWERFUL CENTRE APPLICATIONS
(Of the A B C Core Systems Thinking Technology)

1	**Strategic Management System** (Yearly Cycle)	• Planning • Leadership • Change
2	**Reinventing Strategic Planning** (Always Tailored to Your Needs)	• Comprehensive Strategic Planning • Quick Strategic Planning • Micro Strategic Planning
3	**Cascade of Planning** A Suite of Consistent Planning Technologies	• 3-Year Business Planning • Annual Planning • Strategic Marketing & Sales Planning • Strategic Human Resources Planning • Positioning for Competitive Advantage • Strategic Career & Life Planning
4	**Enterprise-Wide Change** A Suite of Consistent and Seamless Change Technologies ("Watertight/Airtight Integrity")	• Enterprise-Wide Change Management • Strategic Plan—Cascade of Implementation • Culture Change • Leadership Development As A System • Creating Customer Value • Go Innovate! —A System of Innovation • Organizations As High-Performance Systems • Strategic Project Management • Performance Excellence (Building on Baldrige)
5	**Specific Intervention Tools:** **Total Integrated Systems Solutions** An Integrated Suite of Specific, Synergistic, and Practical Applications	• A Suite of Assessment Tools—Online • Daily Problem Solving • Recruiting & Hiring • Succession Planning • Effective Team Work • Performance Management • Process Improvement • Customer Service • Total Quality Management • Customer/Market Focused • Six Levels of Leadership Competencies • 36+ Courses—Leadership & Management Development • Six Levels of People Edge Best Practices • 360° Feedback—Business & Leadership Competencies

(Left margin, vertical text): CASCADE OF CONSISTENCY – "FIT"

All based on one holistic and seamless construct and foundation:
The science of Systems Thinking—The Systems Thinking Approach™

ebewc02.pmd

1420 Monitor Road • San Diego • California • 92110-1545 • (619) 275-6528 • Fax (619) 275-0324

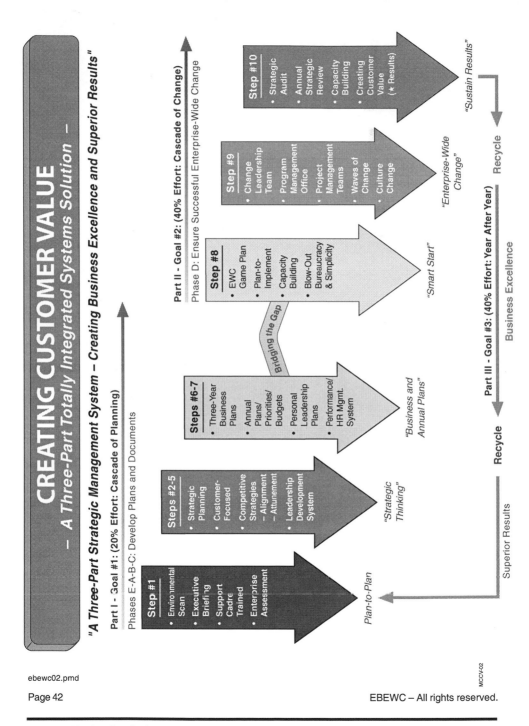

CREATING CUSTOMER VALUE
– A Three-Part Totally Integrated Systems Solution –

"A Three-Part Strategic Management System – Creating Business Excellence and Superior Results"

Part I - Goal #1: (20% Effort: Cascade of Planning)

Phases E-A-B-C: Develop Plans and Documents

Part II - Goal #2: (40% Effort: Cascade of Change)

Phase D: Ensure Successful Enterprise-Wide Change

Part III - Goal #3: (40% Effort: Year After Year)

Business Excellence

Step #1
- Environmental Scan
- Executive Briefing
- Support Cadre Trained
- Enterprise Assessment

Plan-to-Plan

Steps #2-5
- Strategic Planning
- Customer-Focused
- Competitive Strategies
  – Alignment
  – Attunement
- Leadership Development System

"Strategic Thinking"

Steps #6-7
- Three-Year Business Plans
- Annual Plans/ Priorities/ Budgets
- Personal Leadership Plans
- Performance/ HR Mgmt. System

"Business and Annual Plans"

Bridging the Gap

Step #8
- EWC Game Plan
- Plan-to-Implement
- Capacity Building
- Blow-Out Bureaucracy & Simplicity

"Smart Start"

Step #9
- Change Leadership Team
- Program Management Office
- Project Management Teams
- Waves of Change
- Culture Change

"Enterprise-Wide Change"

Step #10
- Strategic Audit
- Annual Strategic Review
- Capacity Building
- Creating Customer Value (★ Results)

"Sustain Results"

Recycle

Recycle

Superior Results

ebewc02.pmd

MCCV-02

1420 Monitor Road • San Diego • California • 92110-1545 • (619) 275-6528 • Fax (619) 275-0324

SECTION III
THE ICEBERG THEORY
OF
ENTERPRISE-WIDE CHANGE

THE ICEBERG

"He who only sees the obvious,
wins his battles with difficulty.
He who sees below the surface of things
wins his battles with ease"

—Sun Tzu

1420 Monitor Road • San Diego • California • 92110-1545 • (619) 275-6528 • Fax (619) 275-0324

Enterprise-Wide Change

Requires a balance in how organizations spend their time and energy between:

1. **Content**/tasks/goals and focus of the business;

2. **Processes** and "how" we go about our behaviors while working on the tasks;

3. The **Structure** (or context/arrangements) within which the content and process operate.

Content   **Process**

Structure

and

It requires persistence, disciplined persistence!

for

Success in Enterprise-Wide Change

The Iceberg Theory of Change

What sinks change efforts are the same things that sink ships:

—The "stuff" below the waterline that is not readily visible.

• In an Iceberg, it is the 87% of the Iceberg below the waterline

• In Organizations, it is the lack of focus on two of the three levels of the "reality of life":

—i.e. Lack of focus on the Underlying processes and Structures needed for effective Change.

1420 Monitor Road • San Diego • California • 92110-1545 • (619) 275-6528 • Fax (619) 275-0324

THE ICEBERG THEORY OF CHANGE
The Systems Thinking Approach™

(The CAPACITY* to Achieve Your Competitive Business Advantage)

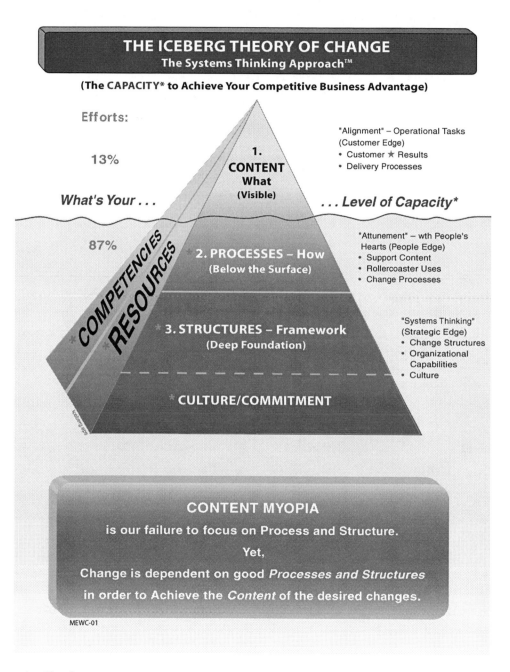

Efforts:

13%

87%

What's Your . . .

. . . Level of Capacity*

1. CONTENT
What
(Visible)

2. PROCESSES – How
(Below the Surface)

3. STRUCTURES – Framework
(Deep Foundation)

CULTURE/COMMITMENT

COMPETENCIES
RESOURCES

"Alignment" – Operational Tasks
(Customer Edge)
• Customer ★ Results
• Delivery Processes

"Attunement" – wth People's
Hearts (People Edge)
• Support Content
• Rollercoaster Uses
• Change Processes

"Systems Thinking"
(Strategic Edge)
• Change Structures
• Organizational
  Capabilities
• Culture

CONTENT MYOPIA

is our failure to focus on Process and Structure.

Yet,

Change is dependent on good *Processes and Structures*

in order to Achieve the *Content* of the desired changes.

MEWC-01

ebewc03.pmd

1420 Monitor Road • San Diego • California • 92110-1545 • (619) 275-6528 • Fax (619) 275-0324

CHANGE PROCESSES STRUCTURES

Why do we need change processes and structures?

It is most difficult for a stable organization to change itself; that is, for the regular structures of the organization to be used for change. They have an investment in the status quo.

Assumptions About the Transition State and Strategic Change

1. All change is a *loss experience* and stress results.

2. There is a *Rational Learning Curve* that people travel at different dates/speeds.

3. There is an *Emotional Rollercoaster* that people also uniquely travel when the stress of change is introduced.

4. People have finite amounts of energy. The **real question** is where do they use their time (i.e., "time is a reflection of one's priorities").

5. The loss experience, the Emotional Rollercoaster, and the Learning Curve all take time and energy . . . instead of productive work time.

6. The political and cultural norms of the organization are high resistance to change and generally defeat a change attempt.

Characteristics of the Change State

- Low stability — ambiguity

- High emotional stress — long hours

- High, often undirected energy/emotions

- Control is a major issue

- Survival behavior

- Conflict increases

Adapted from concepts developed by Kurt Lewin and Richard Beckhardl.

ebewc03.pmd

CHANGE MANAGEMENT CONCEPT

ACHIEVING SUCCESSFUL EXECUTION

The desired changes resulting from Clarity of Purpose will all be fragile.

The desired changes will need to be:

- Nurtured
- Protected
- Encouraged
- Rewarded

The **Enterprise-Wide Change Management Concept** is the only way to accomplish this!

TODAY'S UNDERLYING POWERFUL THEMES OF INNOVATION AND CHANGE

- Fluidity
- Mobility
- Flexibility

- Adaptability
- Individuality
- Customizing

Bright Ideas vs. Persistent Execution

The hard part is the journey;
not
the amount of the destination.

**"The change from the current state
to the future state has traditionally
been underestimated, understaffed, and
inadequately addressed."**
—*Bill Veltrop*

1420 Monitor Road • San Diego • California • 92110-1545 • (619) 275-6528 • Fax (619) 275-0324

INFLUENCE AND STRUCTURE

A ship's captain in Long Beach, California harbor is contacted by a nearby company to deliver some goods to Tokyo, Japan.

Who is the most influential person in this delivery?:

STRUCTURE INFLUENCES BEHAVIOR

Infrastructures are one of the most powerful influences of behavior there are—they are the "context" within which change occurs.

1. Having the right structures in place to begin a change is critical.

2. Desired behaviors need desired structures—both physical and mental/emotional/ cultural.

3. Even colors and shapes and visuals are effective structures.

4. Structures create chain reactions—slow at first, faster later on—Lilypond Theory.

5. Structures need flexibility—too rigid or soft are both bad.

6. In the absence of structures, we create them/they **slowly** emerge.

7. The linkages of the structures to each other are key.

8. Without structures—complacency and chaos rain.

9. Persistence with the structures is key to change.

10. Artificial structures/boundaries can be a mistake.

1420 Monitor Road • San Diego • California • 92110-1545 • (619) 275-6528 • Fax (619) 275-0324

ENTERPRISE-WIDE CHANGE MANAGEMENT

"A MENU" – STRUCTURES AND ROLES

MAIN STRUCTURES – SENIOR LEADERSHIP

1. **Visionary Leadership** — CEO/Senior Executives with **Personal Leadership Plans (PLPs)**
   - For repetitive stump speeches and reinforcement
   - To ensure fit/integration of all parts & people towards the same vision/values
2. **Internal Support Cadre** — Informal/kitchen cabinet
   - For day-to-day coordination of implementation process
   - To ensure the change structures & processes don't lose out to day-to-day
3. **Executive Committee**
   - For weekly meetings and attention
   - To ensure follow-up on the top 15-25 priority yearly actions from the Strategic Plan
4. **Enterprise-Wide Change Leadership Team** (formal)—replaces or is the Strategic Planning Team
   - For bimonthly/quarterly follow-up meetings to track, adjust and refine everything (including the Vision)
   - To ensure follow-through via a yearly comprehensive map of implementation
5. **Program Management Office** — Joint internal and external experts
   - For Enterprise-Wide Change requiring management of multiple change processes and projects
   - To ensure "Watertight Integrity" to your Vision, Positioning, and Values (Strategic Business Design)

SUB-STRUCTURES – PROJECT/PROCESS TEAMS

6. **Strategy Sponsorship/Project or Process Teams**
   - For each core strategy and/or major change effort / Key Initiatives
   - To ensure achievement of each one; including leadership of what needs to change
7. **Employee Development Board** (Attunement of People's Hearts)
   - For succession – careers – development – core competencies (all levels) – performance management/appraisals
   - To ensure fit with our desired values/culture — and employees as a competitive edge
8. **Technology Steering Committee/Group**
   - For computer — telecommunications — software fit and integration
   - To ensure "system-wide" fit/coordination around information management
9. **Strategic Communications System (and Structures)**
   - For clear two way dialogue and understanding of the Plan/implementation
   - To ensure everyone is heading in the same direction with the same strategies/values
10. **Measurement and Benchmarking Team**
    - For collecting and reporting of Key Success Measures, especially customers, employees, competitors
    - To ensure an outcome/customer-focus at all times
11. **Accountability and Responsibility System**—all levels
    - For clear and focused 3-year business plans and annual department plans that are critiqued, shared and reviewed, as well as individual performance appraisals
    - To ensure a fit, coordination and commitment to the core strategies and annual top priorities
12. **Whole System Participation Team** (can combine with #8)
    - For input and involvement of all key stakeholders before a decision affecting them is made. Includes Parallel Processes, Search Conferences, Annual Management Conferences, etc.
    - To ensure a critical mass in support of the vision and desired changes
13. **Rewards and Recognition Programs** (can combine with #6)
    - For recognizing and paying people for strategic management accomplishments
    - To ensure reinforcement of the Accountability and Responsibilities System
14. **Organization Redesign Team**
    - For studying and recommending what redesign of the organization is needed
    - To ensure synergy of the strategies, structures, processes, policies, values and culture
15. **Environmental Scanning System**
    - For collecting data from the environment (SKEPTIC)
    - To ensure advance awareness of coming changes to the environment

ebewc03.pmd

1420 Monitor Road • San Diego • California • 92110-1545 • (619) 275-6528 • Fax (619) 275-0324

POSSIBLE EXTERNAL CHANGE STRUCTURES

1. Advisory Board of Directors

2. Strategic Alliances/Partnerships

3. Customer/Vendor Focus Groups

4. Union-Management Committee

5. Community Special Interest Group (SIG) Sessions

6. Community Forums

7. User Groups

8. Industry/Member Conferences

1420 Monitor Road • San Diego • California • 92110-1545 • (619) 275-6528 • Fax (619) 275-0324

EXECUTIVE/EMPLOYEE DEVELOPMENT BOARD (EDB) CONCEPT

"Invest in Your People First"

The people management practices of any organization should be viewed as a system of people flow from hiring, through their careers, and through retirement and/or termination. See the Centre's copyrighted HR Systems Model and Assessment Tools. Making this all happen is the responsibility of senior management; usually best done through an "EDB" (Executive/Employee Development Board) focused solely on this framework and "creating people as a competitive business advantage." *(The "People Edge")*

For example: As a Board, this reinforces senior management's responsibility to carry out your "stewardship" responsibilities towards yourselves and the rest of your employees. The best way to explain this fully is an example (on the next page) from the author's days as an Executive Vice President of Imperial Corporation of America (ICA), a $14 billion financial services company, formerly based in San Diego, California.

In essence, this Executive Stewardship Board is responsible for the Human Resource Management flow and continuity. It is the executive's responsibility to link staffing to business strategy via:

- hiring
- selection (up/lateral)
- succession planning/core competencies
- developmental jobs/experiences
- Leadership Development System
- training: classroom (internal, external)

- organization design/structure
- socio-demographic trends
- employee surveys of satisfaction/360º feedback
- rewards/performance system
- workforce planning

A mechanism/structure of how to achieve management continuity is needed (i.e., a linking pin of Boards):

1. Executive Development Board (EDB)—executive team
2. Management Development Board (MDB)—all department heads/teams
3. Employee Development Committees (EEDC)—all supervisors/section head areas

The desired outcomes include:

Right person — Right job — Right time — Right organization — Right skills!

Sample Monthly Executive Meetings

Week 1	Operational/Business Issues
Week 2	Strategic Planning and Change Process/Status
Week 3	Strategic Change Issues
Week 4	Customer Satisfaction
*Week 5	Executive/Employee Development Board (EDB)
(Quarterly)	Staff, promotion, succession, development – HR Executive as secretary to Senior Management

ebewc03.pmd

1420 Monitor Road • San Diego • California • 92110-1545 • (619) 275-6528 • Fax (619) 275-0324

ENTERPRISE-WIDE CHANGE LEADERSHIP TEAM

Ineffectiveness of Hierarchical "Cascade" Implementation Strategy Alone

The normal "cascade" strategy for implementing change is usually ineffective, because memories remain embedded in the way the organization works after the change. This applies particularly if the change relates to the culture rather than to work practices or systems.

—Dick Beckhard
Changing the Essence

A new way to run your business, giving equal weight to managing desired changes, in addition to the ongoing daily management of the organization.

Purposes

1. To guide and control the implementation of any large scale, organization-wide strategic planning/change efforts undertaken through the "Reinventing Strategic Management Model (Planning and Change) to Creating a High Performance Organization."

2. To coordinate any other major performance improvement projects going on in the organization at the same time; to ensure fit with the time and energy demands of ongoing daily business activities (i.e., *systems fit, alignment, and integrity*).

Criteria for Enterprise-Wide Change Leadership Team Membership

1. Senior management leadership teams for today and the future as well.

2. Informal or formal leaders from parts of the organization that are key to implementation.

3. "Core Steering Group Implementation Staff Support Team", including overall change management coordinator, KSM/ESS coordinators, and internal facilitators.

4. Credible staff who are knowledgeable of the actual Strategic Plan that was developed.

5. Key stakeholders who share your ideal future vision and are willing to actively support it.

ebewc03.pmd

1420 Monitor Road • San Diego • California • 92110-1545 • (619) 275-6528 • Fax (619) 275-0324

CHANGE LEADERSHIP TEAM (STANDARD MEETING AGENDA)

For Enterprise-Wide Change

Note: This interactive Enterprise-Wide Change follow-up day is to include learning, change management, and team building.

1. **Welcome** — Agenda — Logistics — Norms — "Last" To Do List Reviewed
   • Interactive "change" icebreaker (i.e., change is...)
   • Where in the yearly planning Enterprise-Wide Change cycle/map are we?
   • Review status of Enterprise-Wide Change Game Plan

2. **Review Status** of Key Success Measures vs. targets (KSM Coordinator)

3. **Learning Activity**: Conduct communications and interpersonal skills, coaching, presenting, facilitating, team building or other change management/Strategic Systems Thinking skills needed to have the Team work effectively—and for the change to succeed.

4. **Review Core Strategies**, enterprise-wide change projects, and top priority annual action items (Strategic Sponsorship/Innovative Project Teams/presenters—be interactive, questions and answers, etc.)
   • List top 3 successes to celebrate
   • List top 3 issues/concerns and problem solve them if there's a lack of results
   Note: Rollercoaster of Change—Each topic needs to answer three questions:
   a. Where are we as a team on this Rollercoaster?
   b. Where is the rest of the organization? Differences – Location – Department – Level
   c. What actions are needed to bring us all through these desired changes?

5. **Review of Annual Plan Status** (and 3-Year Business/Functional Plans/Status)
   • For each business unit/department, follow-up results obtained

6. **Program Management Office Integrated Change Reports**
   • Maintain the organization's "systems fit, alignment, and integrity" with any other major changes.

7. **Changing Priorities? Environmental Changes?** (SKEPTIC?)
   • What are they? What to do about them?

8. **Deepen Change Management Understanding and Assessment**
   Each meeting cover one new change management tool and apply it to an issue/strategy:
   • Best Practices List
   • Customer-Focused
   • Empowerment Criteria
   • Cross-Functional Teams
   • HR Management Practices
   • Business Excellence Survey
   • "Change Implications" List
   • Menu on Alignment/Attunement
   • Leadership Development Competencies
   • Positioning/Customer Star Results

9. **Communications to Key Stakeholders** (Continue the Parallel Process)
   • In writing plus face-to-face
   • Stump speeches
   • Unit/department meetings also (cascade communications)

10. **Next Steps**
   • To Do List reviewed—assign accountability/timing
   • Next Change Leadership Team meeting—prepare agenda
   • Next year's timetable for our Annual Strategic/Enterprise-Wide Change Review/planning and budgeting cycle?

11. **Process—How did it go?** (Three questions)
   • Both the day and the Enterprise-Wide Change Management process overall

ebewc03.pmd

1420 Monitor Road • San Diego • California • 92110-1545 • (619) 275-6528 • Fax (619) 275-0324

STRATEGIC THINKING — ONE AGENDA MEETINGS

i.e., "Out of the box thinking" — on a major strategic issue
Make your decisions with "informed intuition"

1. **Keep Asking Questions**

   - What is the wildest idea you can think of in this area? What would it take to do it? What would happen if we did it?

   - What is it you can't do now, but if you could, would fundamentally change your business for the better?

   - Who are the competitors? What are they doing? What is the market data?

   - Take a more holistic—or higher level—systems view (supplier ➔ organization ➔ customer)

2. **Do It As:**

   - Pre-planning–discussion, brainstorming of a topic

   - Post-planning–consensus, debrief

   - When stuck

   - To kick off a topic

   - During the year

3. **Hold One Agenda, One Day Meetings on Key "Nuggets"**

   - With only a very small group of key players on the topic (6-8 maximum)

   - Analyze and discuss the topic in depth—from all angles, with good data

   - Focus on dialogue, discovery and learning; less on planning/documentation

1420 Monitor Road • San Diego • California • 92110-1545 • (619) 275-6528 • Fax (619) 275-0324

FOLLOW-UP DEPARTMENT/UNIT MEETINGS

AFTER EACH ENTERPRISE-WIDE CHANGE (EWC) LEADERSHIP TEAM MEETING

Instructions: Following each meeting, the executive should hold both (1) an "all management" meeting; and (2) an "all employee" meeting to cascade the direction, results, and discussions to everyone in a face-to-face setting.

A sample "all management" meeting agenda might be:

How often?	After each EWC meeting
Where?	On site — conference room or training room
How long?	Two and one half hours
When?	2:30 to 5:00 p.m. followed by social hour
Attended by?	All management members of our division/unit/department

Format:

1. Premeeting agenda sent out (results if available plus input on the agenda from our management members).

2. The unit executive kicks off the meeting giving an overview of current issues/happenings in the organization, and items brought up in the EWC meeting (20 minutes).

3. Questions and answers (10 minutes).

4. Each member of the executives' team speaks for 5 minutes on Core Strategy issues related to their areas of responsibility (20 minutes).

5. Round table discussion led by 1-2 key directors/managers on what they are doing in a key Core Strategy area (40 minutes).

6. Questions and answers (30 minutes).

7. Guest speaker from either inside or outside the organization on EWC matters or new learning/skills we need (30 minutes).

8. Wrap up and social hour.

THE PLAYERS OF ENTERPRISE-WIDE CHANGE

Player #1 Change Leaders/Champions:

- The individual or group that recognizes that change is needed and accepts responsibility for initiating the required change. Must include CEO and senior management.

Player #2 Change Consultants/Facilitators/SMEs:

- The individual or group that agrees with the need for change and accepts responsibility for facilitating the required change. Must be SMEs (Subject Matter Experts) on the processes and structures of change.

Player #3 Change Implementers (All Management and All Employees):

- The individuals or groups that understand and accept the need for change and actually implement the desired change within their daily work and behaviors.

(Always includes the Change Leaders/Consultants because they must "walk the talk")

Player #4 Program Management Office: Enterprise-Wide Change:

- Joint internal and external experts (executive and consultant) in Content, Process, Structural Knowledge, and Skills of successful Enterprise-Wide change efforts.

- It requires both an executive and a consultant who are well-respected and have high credibility, reporting directly to the CEO. They must have no other day-to-day responsibilities except the Enterprise-Wide Change effort (e.g., the same way that Boeing builds aircraft to create future business).

- Be sure to provide them, at minimum, with support staff, a financial analyst, space, and a budget.

1420 Monitor Road • San Diego • California • 92110-1545 • (619) 275-6528 • Fax (619) 275-0324

PLAYER #1 LEADERSHIP DEVELOPMENT COMPETENCIES

BEST PRACTICES RESEARCH – State-of-the-Art

Centering Your Leadership	27 Other Authors
1. Enhancing Self-Mastery	1. 27 out of 27 had a similar item
2. Building Interpersonal Relationships	2. 17 out of 27 had a similar item
3. Facilitating Empowered Teams	3. 6 out of 27 had a similar item
4. Collaborating Across Functions	4. 3 out of 27 had a similar item
5. Integrating Organizational Outcomes	5. 13 out of 27 had a similar item
6. Creating Strategic Positioning	6. 9 out of 27 had a similar item

Note:　None had all 6 competencies.

- Only 3 had four competencies
- Only 4 had three competencies

The Centre does not do basic research. We do action research as well as summarize and synthesize the research of others.

We are translators and interpreters of Best Practices Research.

LEADERSHIP DEVELOPMENT IS BANKRUPT!

ebewc03.pmd

1420 Monitor Road • San Diego • California • 92110-1545 • (619) 275-6528 • Fax (619) 275-0324

PLAYER #2 CHANGE CONSULTANTS/SMEs — STAFF SUPPORT TEAM

Enterprise-Wide Change

List Staff Support Team Names:

Support Cadre	Typical Tasks	Name
1. **Planning**	• Enterprise-Wide Change Planning • Business Unit Change Planning • Current State Assessment/Research	
2. **Finance**	• Key Success Measure Coordinator • Budgeting • Current State Assessment/Economics	
3. **Human Resources**	• Performance/Rewards Management • Training and Development	
4. **Communications**	• Updates After Each Meeting • Print Final Game Plan • Communication Plan	
5. **Subject Matter Experts (SMEs)**	• Experts in specific business topics • Internal or External • Project/Process Team Leaders	
6. **Administrative Assistant**	• Logistics/Follow-up • Laptop Minutes/Document Revisions • Drafts Enterprise-Wide Change Game Plan	
7. **Program Management Office:** Internal Coordinator coordinates or does 1-6	**Minimum List** • Parallel Process/Participative Scheme • Internal Facilitator • Coordinates Entire Enterprise-Wide Process • Facilitates/Supports the Strategic Change Leadership Committee	
8. **External Consultant** (Systems Consultant) Program Management Office	• Facilitate Innovative Change Project Teams • Develops Internal Coordinator • Devil's Advocate/Tough Choices • Advisor on all Enterprise-Wide Change • Subject Matter Experts (SME)	

ebewc03.pmd

1420 Monitor Road • San Diego • California • 92110-1545 • (619) 275-6528 • Fax (619) 275-0324

PLAYER #4: PROGRAM MANAGEMENT LEADERSHIP

The External Consultant Role

1. Jointly leads the day-to-day Enterprise-Wide Change structures and processes along with the internal executive leader.

    *   To coordinate integration across multiple projects and processes.

    *   Ensuring innovative Best Practices Results for each project within the overall process.

    *   Gaining the Superior Results and ROI requirements of each Enterprise-Wide Change process.

2. Acts as a "devil's advocate" by posing frank questions on:

    *   following the core values in the Enterprise-Wide Change process.

    *   pushing for concrete decisions, directions, and priorities.

    *   helping the CEO do what needs to be done, based on what the CEO said they want to achieve in Enterprise-Wide Change.

    *   challenging the CEO and key people about the issues they are backing away from; helping them make the hard decisions.

    *   moving from Vision to Reality.

3. Constantly crafts and facilitates the Enterprise-Wide Change process jointly with the internal executive, but lets the CEO determine the direction of the changes and their future.

4. Brings mastery-levels expertise—content (business and people) teacher-coach, and process facilitation – with objectivity.

5. Assists your internal staff support team in:

    *   being a teacher to line managers/executives.

    *   assisting the CEO and executives to regularly communicate with the rest of the organization about the Enterprise-Wide Change.

6. Assists you in developing an overall **Leadership Development System (Corporate-Wide Core Competency #1)** tied to your Strategic Direction.

7. Facilitates your Strategic Management process to ensure that you build your first **Strategic Management Yearly Cycle (Corporate-Wide Core Competency #2).**

8. Assists you in implementing the results of the Business Excellence Assessment (Building on Baldrige – Best Practices) to ensure **"Watertight Integrity" to your Vision, Values, and Positioning (Corporate-Wide Core Competency #3).**

ebewc03.pmd

PROGRAM MANAGEMENT DUTIES

– THREE ESSENTIALS –

#1 Ensure all other external consultants and trainers are approved by the Program Management Office so that:

- Only one mental map of an **organization as a system** is used

- The **Big Three Enterprise-Wide Failure Issues** are avoided as much as possible

#2 Provide all external consultants and trainers with a 1-2 day orientation and training program and certify them, at their expense, to ensure:

- They now understand and can link their proposed work to your organization's Strategic Plan and direction (i.e. clarity of purpose and simplicity of execution).

- They learn and use the Systems Thinking Approach™, *the natural way the world works*.

#3 Institute the proper joint oversight of their work with the in-house project leader to ensure the training program above is working:

- Use discretion with **"strategic consistency and operational flexibility"** to ensure no bureaucracy is created

- Report and immediately **correct any issues uncovered** while keeping the change leadership team informed

ebewc03.pmd

1420 Monitor Road • San Diego • California • 92110-1545 • (619) 275-6528 • Fax (619) 275-0324

REQUIRED ORGANIZATIONAL CAPACITY

(To undergo Enterprise-Wide Change Successfully)

Instructions: Rate our current Organizational Capacity to build and sustain EWC on a multi-year basis by the collective leadership and management team as well as all employees.

Scoring: (H—M—L)   Comments:

I. Demonstrated Long-Term Commitment: By the Collective Leadership Team to Culture Change 1. ____ CEO 2. ____ Senior Management 3. ____ Board of Directors 4. ____ Collective Management Team 5. ____ All Employees	1 2 3 4 5
II. Effective change Processes: To facilitate a successful EWC process 6. ____ Parallel Involvement Process 7. ____ Rollercoaster of Change Process 8. ____ Wave after Wave of Change Process 9. ____ HR Best People Policies and Practices 10. ____ Strategic Communications Processes	6 7 8 9 10
III. Effective Change Infrastructures: In place to guide the EWC process 11. ____ Change Leadership Team 12. ____ Program Management Office/ Change Team 13. ____ Yearly Map of Implementation 14. ____ Innovative Process/ Project Teams 15. ____ Positive Work Culture	11 12 13 14 15
IV. High Level of Capabilities and Competencies: To lead the EWC effort effectively 16. ____ Leadership Excellence 17. ____ Business Acumen 18. ____ Daily People Management Practices 19. ____ Systems Thinking Applications (Concepts/Tools) 20. ____ Creativity and Innovation Competencies	16 17 18 19 20
V. Adequate Resources: Devoted exclusively to EWC 21. ____ People 22. ____ Time 23. ____ Money 24. ____ Information/Access 25. ____ Equipment/Support/Facilities	21 22 23 24 25

ebewc03.pmd

1420 Monitor Road • San Diego • California • 92110-1545 • (619) 275-6528 • Fax (619) 275-0324

"YEARLY CYCLE" OF THE ENTERPRISE-WIDE CHANGE (STRATEGIC MANAGEMENT SYSTEM)

(TWO+ YEARS TO INSTITUTIONALIZE ENTERPRISE-WIDE CHANGE)

Date

Date		
June - Year #1	1.	Begin Strategic Planning (Plan-to-Plan: 1 day)
July - Oct	2.	Do Strategic Planning (5-8 days overall)
November	3.	**Develop Annual Work Plans/Budgets***
Jan - Year #2	4.	**Conduct Large Group Dept. Plan Review (1 day)***
Jan	5.	**Smart Start: Conduct Plan-to-Implement (2 days)***
Feb - ongoing	6.	Ongoing Operation of Program Management Office (PMO)
March/April	7.	Monthly Leadership Team Review Session
May/etc.	8.	Monthly Leadership Team Review Session
April-July	9.	**Develop 3-Year Business Plans*** **(for Business Units/Major Support Departments)**
September	10.	Evaluate Plan's Year #1 Success—Rewards based on this
Oct-Dec	11.	**Conduct Annual Strategic Review (& Update: 2-4 days overall)***
Jan - Year #3	12.	Develop Updated Annual Department Work Plans/Budgets
Jan	13.	Conduct Large Group Dept. Plan Review (1 day)
Jan - ongoing	14.	Ongoing Operation of Program Management Office (PMO)
March/April	15.	Monthly Leadership Team Review Session
May/etc.	16.	Monthly Leadership Team Review Session
June - Dec	17.	Institutionalized—Strategic Review/Update Again— *as a way of life*

*These are the steps often missed—resulting in failure to implement your Strategic Plan

ebewc03.pmd

SECTION IV
ROLLERCOASTER OF CHANGE™

Over thirty five years of research
have confirmed that:

All systems in nature follow identical

patterns of growth and change!

© 2000, Leadership, Inc.

1420 Monitor Road • San Diego • California • 92110-1545 • (619) 275-6528 • Fax (619) 275-0324

ROLLERCOASTER OF CHANGE™

"Persevere" — The Key to Strategic Change

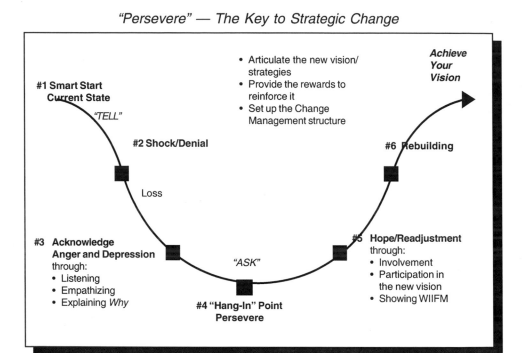

Major Questions

1. Not "if" but "when" will we start to go through shock/depression?
2. How deep is the trough?
3. How long will it take?
4. Will we get up the right (optional) side and rebuild?
5. At what level will we rebuild?
6. How many different rollercoasters will we experience in this change?
7. Are there other changes/rollercoasters occurring?
8. Will we "hang-in" and "persevere" at the midpoint (bottom)? How?
9. How will we deal with normal resistance?
10. How will we create a "critical mass" to support and achieve the change?

ebewc04.pmd

1420 Monitor Road • San Diego • California • 92110-1545 • (619) 275-6528 • Fax (619) 275-0324

LEVELS AND WAVES OF CHANGE IN *THE ROLLERCOASTER OF CHANGE*

–Even If All the Leadership Performs Well–

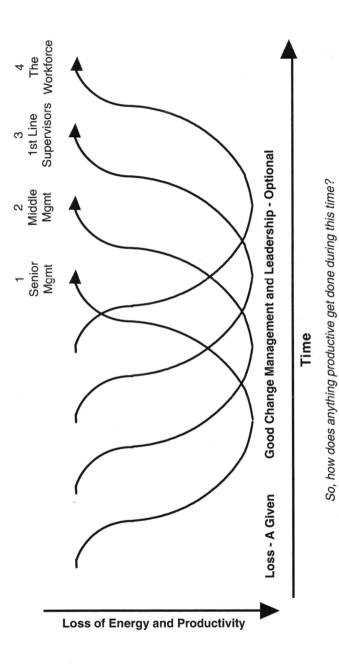

1 Senior Mgmt

2 Middle Mgmt

3 1st Line Supervisors

4 The Workforce

Loss of Energy and Productivity

Loss - A Given

Good Change Management and Leadership - Optional

Time

So, how does anything productive get done during this time?

1420 Monitor Road • San Diego • California • 92110-1545 • (619) 275-6528 • Fax (619) 275-0324

PERSISTENCE . . . HANG IN

"Nothing in the world can take the place of persistence. Talent will not; nothing is more common than unsuccessful men with talent. Genius will not; unrewarded genius is almost a proverb. Education will not; the world is full of educated derelicts. Persistence and determination alone are omnipotent."

Source: Calvin Coolidge

"A basic truth of management — if not of life — is that nearly everything looks like a failure in the middle . . .

. . . persistent, consistent execution is unglamourous, time-consuming, and sometimes boring."

Source: Rosabeth Moss Kanter, July 1990

All Change is a Loss Experience

1. **Loss** creates a feeling of depression for most people. One loses preferred modes of attaining and giving affection, handling aggression, dependency needs—all those *familiar routines* which we have evolved and usually taken for granted.

2. **Loss** is a difficult experience to handle, particularly if what one leaves behind is psychologically important.

3. **All loss** must be mourned and the attendant feelings disgorged if a restitution process is to operate effectively.

4. **Most** organization change flounders because the experience of loss is not taken into account. *To undertake successful organizational change, an executive must anticipate and provide the means of working through that loss and all four phases of it.*

Adapted from Harry Levinson, Psychological Man

ROLLERCOASTER OF CHANGE™

Question: Which concerns do we have in our changes? Circle them. Next, develop strategies to deal with them.

Issues/Concerns	Issues/Concerns
1. Loss of influence	10. Loss of professional identity
2. Loss of control	11. Loss of territory
3. Loss of money	12. Concerns about ability to handle new group
4. Concerns about family reaction to change	13. Loss of role
5. Loss of social status	14. Loss of employment
6. Concerns about starting over— "new kid"	15. Loss of meaning
	16. Concerns about competency
7. Loss of future	17. Fear of failure
8. Loss of relationships, networks	18. Loss of satisfaction
9. Loss of autonomy	19. Loss of support

CHANGING HABITS

"Changing people's habits and way of thinking is like writing your instructions in the snow during a snowstorm. Every 20 minutes you must rewrite your instructions. Only with constant repetition will you create change." —Donald L. Dewar

"The history to mankind is strewn with habits, creeds, and dogmas that were essential to one age and disastrous to another." —James Reston, New York Times columnist

Attitudes: "Attitudes are habits of thinking." —Steve Wilson

Comfortable With Behavior Changes: "It takes 18 months to 2 years of steady disciplined effort to feel comfortable with new behavior." —Harles Cone

ebewc04.pmd

1420 Monitor Road • San Diego • California • 92110-1545 • (619) 275-6528 • Fax (619) 275-0324

TRANSFORMATIONAL CHANGE AND EXCELLENCE

THE FIVE CHOICES OF CHANGE AND LEVELS OF EXCELLENCE

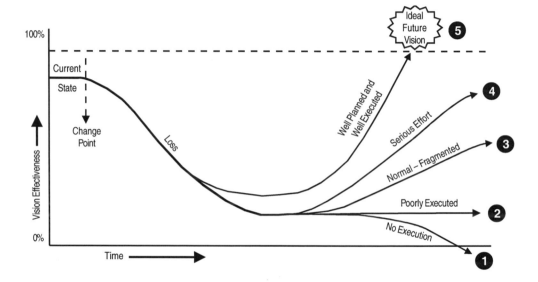

Which will you be?

_____ **1** **Incompetence**—"Going Out of Business"

_____ **2** **Technical** — "Dogged Pursuit of Mediocrity"

_____ **3** **Management** — "Present and Accounted For Only"

_____ **4** **Leadership** — "Making a Serious Effort"

_____ **5** **Visionary Leadership** — "Developing an Art Form"

ebewc04.pmd

1420 Monitor Road • San Diego • California • 92110-1545 • (619) 275-6528 • Fax (619) 275-0324

SOME PRINCIPLES OF CHANGE

The principles of change are research-based; they are not matters of personal opinion.

1. Any change in any one part of the organization affects other parts of the organization—the "Ripple Effect." (An organization is a system and a "web of relationships.") Leaders need constant attention to an integrated fit/alignment and attunement. If not, entropy will take over.

2. People are funny. Change they initiate is viewed as good, needed, and valuable. Change that is forced on them is met by some form of resistance, no matter what the nature of the change.

3. People need predictability—physical, psychological, and social. It's an offshoot of the basic need for security.

4. People will feel awkward, ill-at-ease, and self-conscious; they need information and reassurance over and over again (repetition – repetition – repetition).

5. People will think first about what they will have to give up—their losses; let people cry, mourn and grieve the loss.

6. People will feel alone even though others (everyone) are going through the same change. Structure interactions and involvement for people to feel a sense of community.

7. People also need variety, new experiences, growth, breaks in routine, and creative outlets.

8. The communications power in explicit vision and values is enormous. People want to believe.

9. Only one to three themes (maximum) should be chosen in order to focus people.

10. People change at different rates, depths and speeds; they have different levels of readiness for change.

11. Excellence is doing 10,000 little things rights—that's strategic management in execution.

12. "Structures" exist—their design influences everything else.

13. "Processes" exist—only issue is their focus and effectiveness.

14. There is a need for a continual "change management" process—the hierarchal organization has a difficult time changing itself.

continued

ebewc04.pmd

1420 Monitor Road • San Diego • California • 92110-1545 • (619) 275-6528 • Fax (619) 275-0324

SOME PRINCIPLES OF CHANGE

15. The stress of change on people is enormous . . . but can and must be managed for successful change to occur. People can only handle so much change; don't overload—it causes paralysis.

16. Being open to feedback doesn't have to be a sacred cow . . . but it can be painful; yet grow inducing, as you have more of reality with which to improve.

17. Employees can be a bottom line competitive business advantage—but only if management first becomes the advantage.

18. People will be concerned they don't have enough resources; help them get "outside the 9 Dots."

19. If you take pressure for change off, people will revert back to old behaviors; relapses are natural and will occur.

20. We rarely use what works despite the fact that proven research is in on change management.

21. What else?

Adapted from John Laurie, Ken Blanchard, Bill Pfeiffer, and Steve Haines

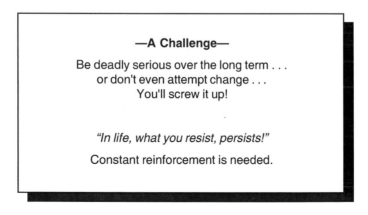

—A Challenge—

Be deadly serious over the long term . . .
or don't even attempt change . . .
You'll screw it up!

"In life, what you resist, persists!"

Constant reinforcement is needed.

ebewc04.pmd

1420 Monitor Road • San Diego • California • 92110-1545 • (619) 275-6528 • Fax (619) 275-0324

WAYS TO UNFREEZE AN ORGANIZATION

(INDUCE PHASES 2 AND 3: SHOCK/DENIAL AND ANGER/ DEPRESSION)

1. Share what competitors are doing.

2. Explain your organization's finances and P/L statement.

3. Share your organization's vision and future ideal.

4. Clarify the impact on the organization and employees of a particular situation or issue.

5. Conduct an organizational survey. Feed it back to "X."

6. Collect interview data and feed it back to "X."

7. Re-explain job expectations/standards of performance.

8. Change the reward system (individual – team – organization-wide).

9. Discuss changes in the environment that impact the organization.

10. Discuss why there is a need to change.

11. Explain the organization's strategic plans and direction and why they are chosen.

12. Set goals with employees.

13. Examine employee data, such as turnover, etc.

14. Conduct an unfiltered upward feedback meeting.

15. Change the roles of key informal leaders.

16. Feed back customer perceptions and data.

17. Conduct focus groups of employees or customers.

18. Change the location of management offices to be closer to the workers.

19. Set up task forces to analyze issues and recommend solutions.

20. Explicitly evaluate employees (including senior management) on your espoused values.

ebewc04.pmd

1420 Monitor Road • San Diego • California • 92110-1545 • (619) 275-6528 • Fax (619) 275-0324

FACTORS NEEDED TO GO THROUGH THE STAGES OF CHANGE SUCCESSFULLY

(SPECIFICALLY PHASES 2 AND 3: DEPRESSION/ANGER AND HOPE/ADJUSTMENT)

1. This is a time of high uncertainty and anxiety.
    a. Communicate frequently downward about the change and change process.
    b. Develop feedback mechanisms to hear the employees' questions and concerns and then a way to conduct two-way dialogues.
2. Don't react emotionally to employee concerns and resistance. Empathize and understand it. Let people talk it out. Then try to deal with the underlying issues (i.e., read between the lines.)
3. Let people have a clear understanding of why the change is necessary.
4. Let people have an opportunity to critically cross-examine the leader(s) and verify for themselves the necessity for change.
5. Give people occasions to talk through their feelings of loss and detachment from the old ways.
6. Have methods by which people affected by the change can participate in some aspect of change to control their destiny.
7. Have management develop and organize new support systems to establish the new state.
8. Develop a positive climate about the change by evoking a clear and positive "common vision" of what the end state of the change will look like.
9. Show people how the change can personally help them and their needs.
10. Relate the change to employee values.
11. Develop teams—not just groups or departments—and a value and a reward for teamwork.
12. Work closely with the informal leaders of the organization.
13. Provide employees with an opportunity to increase their learning and competence about their jobs and about the change.
14. Develop and communicate about your well-planned "transition management process" to give employees a sense of security and knowledge that you are in control and in charge of the changes.

ebewc04.pmd

1420 Monitor Road • San Diego • California • 92110-1545 • (619) 275-6528 • Fax (619) 275-0324

WAYS TO INSTITUTIONALIZE CHANGES IN AN ORGANIZATION

(PHASE 6 – REBUILDING)

Refreezing/Renewing and Maintaining

Stability/Flexibility in an Organization

Note: While it may be good to think of institutionalizing change in an organization, the practical reality is that once you institutionalize this new changed state, you will immediately begin to make other incremental changes in response to changing conditions. This continues indefinitely! (i.e., continual improvement/renewal).

There are ways to insure changes are successfully completed and maintained. They include:

1. Conduct an organizational assessment to see the status of the change and problems that need improvement in order for the change to reach its full effectiveness.

2. Conduct refresher training courses on the change topic.

3. Hold yearly conferences on the subject (renewal).

4. Have the basic change and also the improvements listed in #1 above as part of senior line management's goals and performance appraisal.

5. Conduct a reward system's diagnosis and make appropriate changes so that the rewards (both financial and non-financial) are congruent and consistent with the changes.

6. Set up an ongoing audit system. Also find ways to statistically measure the change effectiveness. Line managers are used to statistics and generally like them.

7. Have ways to discuss and reinforce the change at periodic staff meetings of top management and department heads.

8. Set the changes into policies and procedures on the ongoing organization; then have someone accountable for them. Set up permanent jobs to maintain the changes or put the accountability into existing job descriptions.

9. Use a variety of communications avenues and processes for both one way and two way feedback on the change.

10. Hold periodic team meetings on the subject across the organization.

ebewc04.pmd

continued

1420 Monitor Road • San Diego • California • 92110-1545 • (619) 275-6528 • Fax (619) 275-0324

WAYS TO INSTITUTIONALIZE CHANGES IN AN ORGANIZATION

11. Have top line managers conduct "deep sensing" meetings on the subject down into the organization on a regular basis.

12. Have periodic intergroup or interdepartmental meetings on the subject and its status.

13. Set up a process of yearly renewing and reexamining the change in order to continually improve it.

14. Have outside consultants conduct periodic visits on the subject and assess the status of the change.

15. Be doubly sure that the top team continues to model the changes. (You can refreeze this through many of the other items on this total list.)

16. Set priorities and deadlines for short-term improvements to the change.

17. Look closely at the key environmental sectors to be sure they are reinforcing the changes (particularly any parent companies or division heads).

18. Create physical indications of the permanency of the change (offices, jobs, brochures, etc.)

19. Develop "stay agents" or multiple persons who have a strong interest in maintaining the change (particularly among line managers and the informal leaders).

20. Refine change procedures to make them routine and normal.

21. Link other organizational systems to the change. Encourage specific and formal communications, coordination, and processes between them.

22. Keep the goals and benefits of the change clear and well known.

23. Assess the potential dangers and pitfalls of the change and develop specific approaches and plans to minimize these dangers.

24. Be alert to other changes that can negatively affect this change. (Unintended negative side effects and consequences).

25. Have a different person manage the stability than the one who managed the change. They are different tasks involving people with different personalities. Change agents are poor stay agents!

1420 Monitor Road • San Diego • California • 92110-1545 • (619) 275-6528 • Fax (619) 275-0324

SIX STAGES OF ENTERPRISE-WIDE CHANGE™
"The Transformation to Business Excellence and Superior Results"

"The Rollercoaster is Natural – Normal – and Highly Predictable"

Vision

Strategic Change
Annual Review

#6 - Rebuilding
Climb the Learning Curve
Begin Getting Results
(Feedback/Follow-up/Culture Change)

#5 - Hope/Readjustment
Reestablish Direction/Begin Future Planning
Focus on Strategic Initiatives and Integration
(Coordinated Enterprise-Wide Change)

*Integrated Change
Is Optional*

"ASK"

#4 - "Hang In" Persevere
New Team Start Up – Build Innovative Teams
(Reorganize Work Responsibilities)

Throughout:
- Articulate the New Vision/
  Values/Strategies
- Provide the Rewards to Reinforce it
- Set up the Change
  Management Structures

"TELL"

*Loss Is
A Given*

#1 - Smart Start
Pre-Planning
(Get Ready/Educated)

#2 - Shock/Denial
Kick-off - Lead Change
(Comm. Change)

#3 - Anger & Depression
Make Changes - Re-Design
(Deal with Loss, Resistence, and Unfreezing)

USING THE BUSINESS EXCELLENCE ARCHITECTURE

(1) Culture (2) Planning (3) Change (4) People (5) Leadership (6) Customer-Focused (7) Align Delivery = CREATING CUSTOMER VALUE

ebewc04.pmd

MEWC-03

1420 Monitor Road • San Diego • California • 92110-1545 • (619) 275-6528 • Fax (619) 275-0324

SIX NATURAL PHASES OF CHANGE

PHASES	GOALS AND MAJOR ACTIONS
I. Smart-Start	**I. Pre-Planning: Goal–Be ready to lead and manage the change effectively.** A. Finalize the decisions about the changes. B. Conduct "Plan-to-Implement" (structures, roles, processes, phases). C. Plan out the announcement details of the actual change decision in "military precision."
II. Shock/Denial	**II. Kick-Off the Change: Goal–To communicate the changes.** A. Communicate the changes openly, along with their rationale, in a "TLC" fashion. Treat people with dignity and respect. B. "Unfreeze" the organization from the old, steady state, using proven techniques to do so. C. Minimize, as much as possible, the inducement and sense of shock, denial and loss.
III. Anger/Depression	**III. Reorganize People: Goal–Deal effectively with the losses, concerns and emotions people naturally feel.** A. Begin to implement the changes in people, jobs, structures, processes, severance, etc. B. Deal effectively with the anger, depression and loss, using proven techniques to do so. C. Continually explain the vision as well as the logic and rationale behind it as to why the change is occurring and necessary.
IV. Hang-In/Persevere	**IV. New Team Start Up: Goal–Clarify new work/team roles and responsibilities.** A. Communicate the expectations and style of the new structures and supervisors. B. Clarify roles and responsibilities of each new team member as well as answer "WIIFM" for each person. C. Decide and agree on new team operational procedures and processes. Begin to build relationships.
V. Hope/Adjustment	**V. Re-Establish the New Direction and Management Systems: Goal–Decide, agree, and communicate plans for the future.** A. Rebuild all management processes and systems to Blow out Bureaucracy and Waste and serve the customer better. B. Redo strategic, business and operational plans and budgets; all based on the desire marketplace positioning and changes in strategy/vision. C. Reinforce desired cultural changes through employee involvement and participation in decisions that affect them.
VI. Rebuild	**VI. Climb the Learning Curve: Goal–Become a high performance organization.** A. Conduct follow-up team building and improve cross-functional teamwork to achieve your vision. B. Gather customer feedback and take needed actions to improve customer value. C. Conduct employee surveys and make changes needed to ensure you live the desired values and culture.

ebewc04.pmd

1420 Monitor Road • San Diego • California • 92110-1545 • (619) 275-6528 • Fax (619) 275-0324

ENTERPRISE-WIDE CHANGE AND TRADITIONAL O.D.– ORGANIZATION DEVELOPMENT CUBE

A SCHEME FOR CLASSIFYING AND CLARIFYING CHANGE PROJECTS
(Roles, System Levels, Diagnosis)

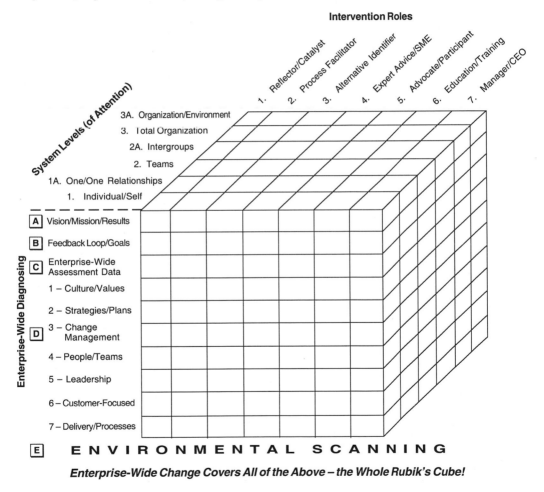

Enterprise-Wide Change Covers All of the Above – the Whole Rubik's Cube!

1420 Monitor Road • San Diego • California • 92110-1545 • (619) 275-6528 • Fax (619) 275-0324

CHANGE INITIATIVES ALREADY UNDERTAKEN

Target Ring	Initiative(s)	Results?
1. **Intrapersonal** (Individual)		
1a. **Interpersonal** (One-to-One)		
2. **Teams** (Departments-Units)		
2a. **Cross-Functional Teams** (Projects)		
3. **Organization-Wide**		
3A. **Organization-Envlronment**		

ebewc04.pmd

Page 78

1420 Monitor Road • San Diego • California • 92110-1545 • (619) 275-6528 • Fax (619) 275-0324

SECTION V
COMMUNICATIONS

**Communicate – Communicate – Communicate
Involvement – Involvement – Involvement**

Main Premise #2

"People support
what they help create."

#3. Range of Participative	
Management/Leadership	
#2. Abdicate	#1. Autocrat

So it follows:

*Involve people in decisions that affect them . . .
prior to the decision being made.*

Skeptics are my best friends!

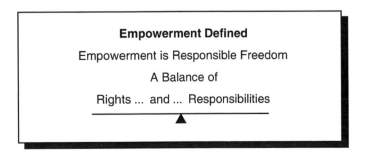

Empowerment Defined

Empowerment is Responsible Freedom

A Balance of

Rights ... and ... Responsibilities

ebewc05.pmd

1420 Monitor Road • San Diego • California • 92110-1545 • (619) 275-6528 • Fax (619) 275-0324

"People Support What They Help Create"

KEY STAKEHOLDER ASSESSMENT

1. Who are all our stakeholders (both Internal and External)? Be specific:

INTERNAL	EXTERNAL

2. Decide who are the top 5-7 stakeholders in terms of importance to the success (both plus and minus) of our Strategic Planning and Enterprise-Wide Change process.

ebewc05.pmd

1420 Monitor Road • San Diego • California • 92110-1545 • (619) 275-6528 • Fax (619) 275-0324

PARALLEL INVOLVEMENT PROCESS
"People Support What They Help Create"

INSTEAD OF D.A.D.: Decide, Announce, Defend

SET UP THE PLANNING & CHANGE COMMUNITY

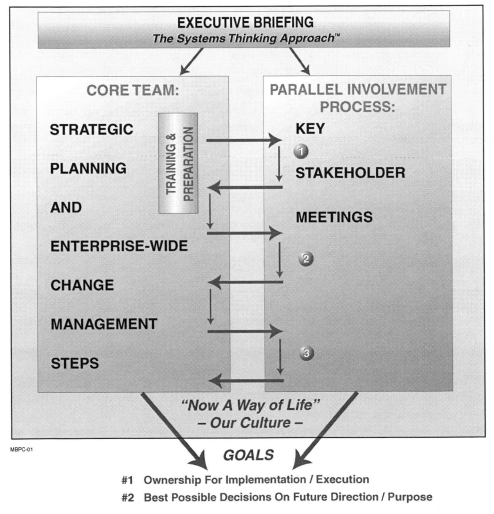

MBPC-01

GOALS

#1 Ownership For Implementation / Execution

#2 Best Possible Decisions On Future Direction / Purpose

ebewc05.pmd

1420 Monitor Road • San Diego • California • 92110-1545 • (619) 275-6528 • Fax (619) 275-0324

PARALLEL INVOLVEMENT PROCESS MEETINGS

PURPOSE (AND AGENDA)

1. To explain the Strategic Planning / Enterprise-Wide Change effort and your role/ involvement in it.
2. To understand the draft documents clearly.
3. To give us input and feedback to take back to the full core planning team.

   • **Guarantee**: Your feedback will be seriously considered.

   • **Limitation**: Input is being gathered from many different people. Therefore, it is impossible for each person's input to be automatically placed in the final document exactly as desired.

OVERALL MEETING PURPOSE

1. This is an **information sharing and input/feedback** meeting.
2. It is **not a decision-making meeting**. This will be done by the Core Planning/ Enterprise-Wide Team at their next meeting, based on your feedback.

THE "MAGIC" IS IN THE ITERATION

How to get the best answers?

1. **Creativity and Innovation come from:**
   • intense dialogue/thought
   • time to get away/reflect—doing your day-to-day job
   • a second or even third intense dialogue
     – in the Parallel Process
     – in the next planning meeting

2. **Testing via the Parallel Involvement Process is the crucible to:**
   • improve the quality of the answers
   • develop "buy in" and commitment to the answer

The Question is—*When are you "ready" for closure?*

ebewc05.pmd

1420 Monitor Road • San Diego • California • 92110-1545 • (619) 275-6528 • Fax (619) 275-0324

20-60-20 Rule – Bell-Shaped Curve

The most important rule to keep in mind when you're facing a change effort is the 20-60-20 rule:

- That approximately 20% of the people in the organization will be change friendly;

- The next 60% will sit on the fence;

- and the remaining 20% will resist, or even deliberately try to make it fail.

That means you have a heavy burden—because only 20% of the people will be with you from the start—so you must pull the other 80% of the organization toward your company's new goals.

–Deloitte and Touche
Personnel Journal, July 1996

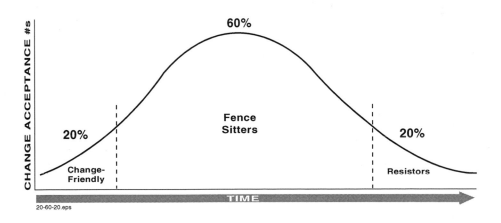

20-60-20.eps

ebewc05.pmd

1420 Monitor Road • San Diego • California • 92110-1545 • (619) 275-6528 • Fax (619) 275-0324

IMPORTANCE OF MIDDLE MANAGERS

As chief executives strive to get their companies to think strategically, they are discovering the importance of their line managers, especially their middle managers. That's right, middle managers — the Rodney Dangerfields of corporate America. Reshuffled, depowered, and pensioned off during the past decade, they are reemerging as the missing link in the drive to turn visions into realities. Says Jeanie Duck, a vice-president at Boston Consulting Group in Chicago:

"I am frankly amazed at the number of companies I see where people don't know what the strategies are. The CEOs have ennobled the worker. Now they're asking, 'What about the middle manager?'"

Source: Ronald Henkoff, *Fortune*, December 31, 1990

Big Transition Task

To re-frame middle management's perceived loss of power

From: Boss to Coach
From: Manager to (also) Leader

PEOPLE TO BE INVOLVED IN THE CHANGE EFFORT:

1.　People with information

2.　People with influence in the organization (informal leaders)

3.　People impacted by the change

4.　People with resources to make the change happen

5.　Collective leadership of the organization

ebewc05.pmd

1420 Monitor Road • San Diego • California • 92110-1545 • (619) 275-6528 • Fax (619) 275-0324

HOW TO BUILD A CRITICAL MASS

TEN WAYS (THE LILY POND THEORY)

It can take two years to build your critical mass. The following are ways to help you do this:

1. Modify Strategic Plan/Enterprise-Wide Change drafts — listen, review (i.e., the Parallel Process).

2. Continue to hold Parallel Involvement Process meetings with key stakeholders throughout implementation.

3. Develop trust in your leadership by being open via the Change Leadership Team, Program Management Office and every day — involve skeptics.

4. Developing 3-year Business Plans for all Business Units/Major Support Departments by involving key stakeholders/staff.

5. Develop Annual Plans for all departments/divisions/sections under the Strategic Plan/core strategy umbrella.

6. Put out "updates" after each Change Leadership Team meeting and ask for feedback.

7. Use Innovative Project/Process Teams and/or Strategic Sponsorship Teams as "change agents" and Implementation Vehicles for each core strategy and key initiatives.

8. Implement quick changes/actions so people know you are serious (silent majority).

9. Review reward systems and the performance appraisal form to reinforce core values and core strategies.

10. Answer WIIFM for each person (i.e., political–cultural issues)

Remember that "skeptics are our best friends." If you encounter skeptics during your Parallel Involvement Process, be sure to ask them why they are skeptical. Get them to identify the roadblocks; don't try to force them to agree with you. Those roadblocks are the key items to be sure to overcome to ensure successful achievement of your vision.

Critical Mass Building – It takes almost 2 years to build enough support (i.e., Lily Pads) in an organization (i.e., Lily Pond) to create the critical mass.

Year #1
- Core Strategic Planning/Enterprise-Wide Team
- plus 20-40 key "others"

Year #2
- the rest of the organization
- other key external stakeholders

ebewc05.pmd

IDEAS FOR INITIALLY COMMUNICATING THE ENTERPRISE-WIDE CHANGE GAME PLAN

- Print the plan and distribute it with a cover letter (KISS). Tri-fold on Strategic Plan – One page KSM matrix – One-page Annual Plan Priorities – One-page Yearly Map of Implementation.

- Develop handouts/overhead slides for "standard use" by all executives.

- Hold organization-wide managers meeting to hear directly from the CEO/Executive Director and other members of the planning team. (Also thank them for their help.)

- Hold divisional/department all-employee meetings to ask questions about the plan and pose concerns.

- Hold stakeholder meetings to review results and thank them for their help.

- Hold two-day workshops to learn about strategic planning, to discuss the strategic plan, and to build supporting plans at a unit/site or individual level.

- Require "Strategic Business Planning" process for units/major support functions.

- Develop posters with planning themes.

- Print up individual (plastic) cards with values, mission, and KSMs.

- Make video tapes of the CEO/Executive Director or others explaining the organization's vision and strategies to achieve that vision.

- Publish internal newsletter stories or memos/letters introducing the plan (overall, and then again one piece at a time).

- Publish external news releases and special public feature stories.

- Do *report cards* each quarter — shared with all stakeholders.

> **Now— how to keep the Plan alive over the next 3-5 years?**

> People don't fail in planning,
> they fail in implementation.
>
> ## *Why?*
>
> Well, my fundamental belief is that they fail because of the lack of ability to get people involved and committed.

Goal #1

E Environment Scan

A Positioning Values

B Measures Goals

Revolutionary Change

To affect real change, a business must overhaul its basic assumptions about its internal and external environment.

CLARITY OF PURPOSE DEFINITIONS

(CREATE YOUR OWN FUTURE)

1. **Vision: Aspirational — Idealistic** *"Our Guiding Star"*
    - Our view/image of what the ideal future looks like at time "X"
    - It has dreamlike qualities, future hopes and *aspirations,* even if they are never fully attainable
    - An energizing, positive, and inspiring statement of *where and what we want to be* in the future

2. **Mission: Pragmatic — Realistic** *"Our Unique Purpose"*
    - What business are we in? (not the activities we do)
    - **"Why we exist** — our reason for being" (raison d' être)
    - The purpose towards which we commit our work life
    - **What we produce**; its' benefits/outcomes
    - **Who we serve** — our customers/clients

3. **Core Values: Our Beliefs** *"What We Believe In"*
    - How do we/should we act while accomplishing this business/mission?
    - "The way we do our business" — *our process*
    - Principles that guide our daily behaviors
    - What we believe in and how we will act at work

4. **Positioning: Our Driving Force — Distinctiveness** *"Our Competitive Edge"*
    - Grand strategy–Strategy–Strategic Intent–competitive advantage
    - What uniquely positions us as different or better in the marketplace vs. the competition that causes the customer to do business with us = **Customer Value**

    "Our Memorizable Essence"
5. **Rallying Cry: Our Essence — Motivational Force**
    - The crisp slogan (8 words or less) that is remembered by the employees and is *the essence* of the vision, mission, and core values (i.e., our driving force/ positioning upon which all else revolves)
    - It should be a powerful motivational force for our staff as it is memorable, memorized, believable, repeatable and **lived on a daily basis across the organization** — everywhere and in every way

ebewc06.pmd

1420 Monitor Road • San Diego • California • 92110-1545 • (619) 275-6528 • Fax (619) 275-0324

CREATING CUSTOMER VALUE: POSITIONING

Anticipating Customers' Wants and Needs
For Products, Services and the Intangibles
Through the Systems Thinking Approach™

Perceived Customer Value = $\dfrac{\text{Outputs}}{\text{Inputs}}$ = Multiple Outcomes

Question: What does this Star mean to you? Define it in your words.

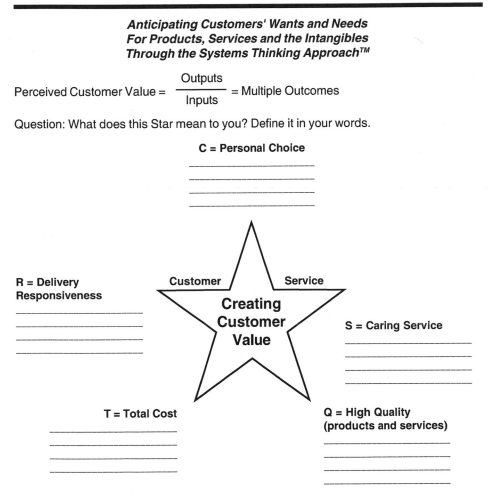

C = Personal Choice

_____
_____
_____
_____

R = Delivery Responsiveness

_____
_____
_____
_____

Customer   Service

Creating Customer Value

S = Caring Service

_____
_____
_____
_____

T = Total Cost

_____
_____
_____
_____

Q = High Quality (products and services)

_____
_____
_____
_____

Question: Which level of competitiveness are you (1, 2, or 3) on each of the five factors?

Level #1 - Competitive Edge
Level #2 - Competitive
Level #3 - Uncompetitive

ebewc06.pmd

1420 Monitor Road • San Diego • California • 92110-1545 • (619) 275-6528 • Fax (619) 275-0324

GUIDING PRINCIPLES FOR ENTERPRISE-WIDE CHANGE™

These Core Values are the ones that seem to work best as Guiding Principles for a successful Enterprise-Wide Change process.

1. **Creativity and Innovation**
   - Learning and Knowledge Transfer
   - Flexibility and Adaptability

2. **Teamwork and Participation/Involvement**
   - Relationships and Commitments
   - Sharing and Connectedness

3. **Holistic and Systemic Orientation**
   - Elegant Simplicity
   - Strategic Thinking

4. **Accountability and Responsibility**
   - Openness and Feedback
   - Courage and Integrity

5. **Customer and Service-Oriented**
   - Speed and Responsiveness

ebewc06.pmd

1420 Monitor Road • San Diego • California • 92110-1545 • (619) 275-6528 • Fax (619) 275-0324

ATTUNEMENT WITH PEOPLE'S HEARTS AND MINDS

CORE VALUES ASSESSMENT AND USES THROUGHOUT ALL FOUR PHASES OF A HIGH PERFORMING ORGANIZATION

The following are typical categories where Core Values should appear and be reinforced within an organization. Where else should they appear and be reinforced in your organization?

A 1. **Strategic Plan**

- Explicit corporate philosophy/values statement—visuals on walls; in rooms

B 2. **Feedback**

- This analysis
- Employee Survey
- 360° Feedback

C 3. **Links to Strategies**

- Annual Department Plan Actions
- Performance evaluation; appraisal forms (assess values adherence); team rewards

Alignment of Delivery Processes

D₁ 4. **Operational Tasks/Processes**

- Corporate and product advertising
- New customers and suppliers vs. current customer and supplier treatment and focus (vs. values)
- Operational processes resulting in quality and service

5. **Structure**

- Dealing with difficult times/issues (i.e., layoffs, reorganizations)
- Organization and job design questions

6. **Resources/Technology/Communications**

- Internal communication (vehicles/publications)
- Press releases, external publications/brochures
- Image nationwide (as seen by others)
- Resource allocation decisions

Attunement of People's Hearts and Minds

D₂ 7. **Leadership**

- Flow of orientation and assimilation versus sign-up
- Job aids/descriptions
- New executive start-up
- To whom and how promotions occur (values consequence assessed); criteria
- Executive leadership ("walk the talk"); ethical decisions; how we manage

8. **HR Processes and Practices**

- Recruiting handbook; selection criteria
- How applicants are treated (vs. values)
- How "rewards for performance" operates (vs. values), especially nonfinancial rewards
- Role of training; training programs (vs. values)
- Policies and procedures (HR, finance, administrative, etc.); day-to-day decisions

9. **Teams**

- Cross-departmental events, flows, tasks forces/teams

Enterprise-Wide Change Management Process

D₃ 10. **Macro**

- Managing change (according to values)
- Stakeholder relationships (vs. values)

ebewc06.pmd

1420 Monitor Road • San Diego • California • 92110-1545 • (619) 275-6528 • Fax (619) 275-0324

THE QUADRUPLE BOTTOM LINE™ = BALANCE

The Systems Thinking Approach™ to Key Success Measures (KSMs)

1. Employees
   a. Operations

2. Customers

3. Stockholders (Owners)

4. Stakeholders (Community/Society)

Note: The popular "Balanced Scorecard" concept is not a systems approach, but it covers some of the same KSM areas that we do, especially 1, 2, and 3.

Holistic View—Key Success Measures

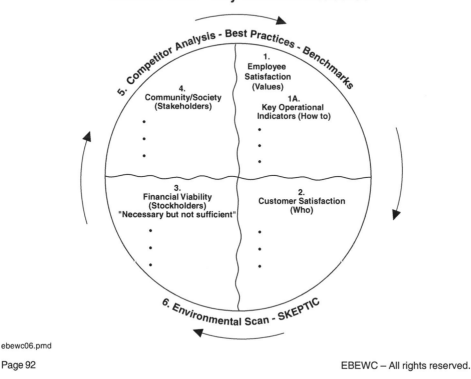

1420 Monitor Road • San Diego • California • 92110-1545 • (619) 275-6528 • Fax (619) 275-0324

THE CASCADE OF PLANNING™
The Systems Thinking Approach™

"STRATEGIC CONSISTENCY AND OPERATIONAL FLEXIBILITY"

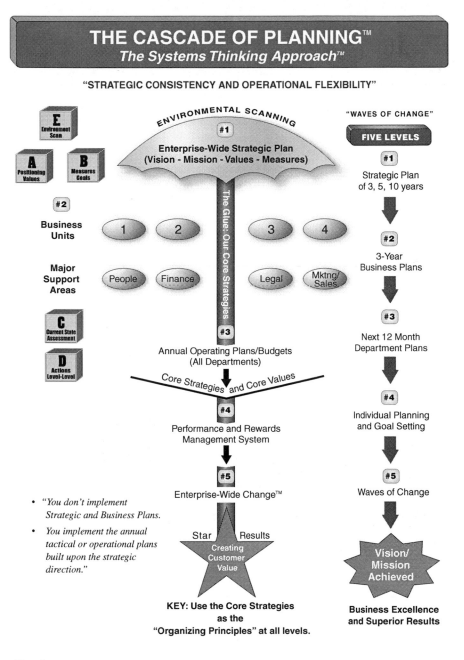

- *"You don't implement Strategic and Business Plans.*
- *You implement the annual tactical or operational plans built upon the strategic direction."*

KEY: Use the Core Strategies as the "Organizing Principles" at all levels.

Business Excellence and Superior Results

1420 Monitor Road • San Diego • California • 92110-1545 • (619) 275-6528 • Fax (619) 275-0324

STRATEGIES, ANNUAL PLANS, AND BUDGETS

(Two-Page Corporate Yearly "Cheat Sheet" and To Do List)

Instructions: In terms of ensuring our overall success this fiscal year, **what are the top three-four priority action items for each core strategy** which need to be accomplished?

Core Strategies	Who Responsible?	When Done?
Core Strategy #1: _____ 1. 2. 3. 4.		
Core Strategy #2: _____ 1. 2. 3. 4.		
Core Strategy #3: _____ 1. 2. 3. 4.		
Core Strategy #4: _____ 1. 2. 3. 4.		
Core Strategy #5: _____ 1. 2. 3. 4.		
Core Strategy #6: _____ 1. 2. 3. 4.		
Coro Strategy #7: _____ 1. 2. 3. 4.		

ebewc06.pmd

1420 Monitor Road • San Diego • California • 92110-1545 • (619) 275-6528 • Fax (619) 275-0324

ANNUAL PLAN FORMAT
(AND FUNCTIONAL/DIVISION/DEPARTMENT PLANS ALSO)

Date: _____

Fiscal Year: _____

#1 Strategies/Themes/Goals: (What) _____

Yearly Pri #	Strategic Action Items (Actions/Objectives/How?)	Support/ Resources Needed	Who Responsible?	Who Else to Involve?	When Done?	Optional How to Measure?	Status

ebewc06.pmd

1420 Monitor Road • San Diego • California • 92110-1545 • (619) 275-6528 • Fax (619) 275-0324

LARGE GROUP ANNUAL DEPARTMENT REVIEWS

(AND LARGE GROUP – WHOLE SYSTEM – TEAM BUILDING)

Tasks:
1. *Small group* presentations by all major department heads (# = _____)
    —on their Department Annual Work Plans.
2. To the "collective" leadership/management of the entire organization (# = _____).

Large Ballroom:

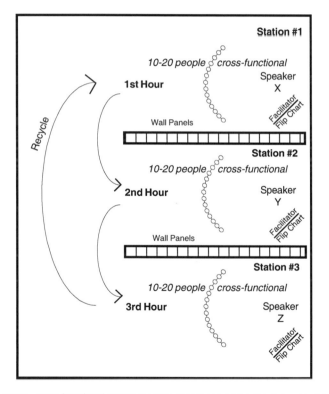

Philosophy: Small group, cross-functional teams meeting together and moving around in hourly activities create greater interaction, more energy, commitment, understanding, buy-in and teamwork to implement the Strategic Plan.

Large group "dog and pony" presentations are boring at best!

ebewc06.pmd

1420 Monitor Road • San Diego • California • 92110-1545 • (619) 275-6528 • Fax (619) 275-0324

PERFORMANCE APPRAISALS . . . KISS

TIED TO STRATEGIC PLANNING

Performance Appraisals
must be tied to support
#1
Your organization's Core Strategies (i.e., results)
and
#2
Your organization's Core Values (i.e., behaviors)
and
#3
Your own learning and growth (i.e., career development)
(If you are serious about your Strategic Plan)

— **Result: A Four Page Performance Management/Appraisal Form** —

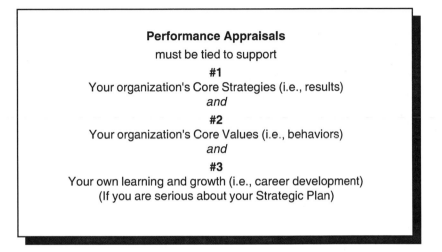

❶ Cover Sheet	❷ Results		❸ Values		❹ Career Development	
	Strategies	Plan/ Actual	Values	Plan/ Actual	Objectives	Action Plan
	1.		1.		1. **X** : _____	
	2.		2.		_____	
	3.				2. **Y** : _____	
Summary	4.		3.		_____	
Evaluation	5.		4.		3. **Z** : _____	
					_____	

ebewc06.pmd

1420 Monitor Road • San Diego • California • 92110-1545 • (619) 275-6528 • Fax (619) 275-0324

CASCADE #1: ENTERPRISE-WIDE LEADERSHIP

FIRST:

> **CLARITY OF PURPOSE (Enterprise-Wide Change Vision or Strategic Plan)**
> **(Work *ON* the Enterprise)**

THEN:

> **CASCADE #1: ENTERPRISE-WIDE**
> **(Work *IN* the Enterprise)**

Cascade the Enterprise-Wide Change Journey throughout the organization:

Cascade #1: Shared Core Enterprise-Wide Change Strategies
(Total-Organization Ring)

Cascade #2: Department Change Plans
(Work-Teams Ring)

Cascade #3: Large Group Enterprise-Wide Change Reviews
(One-to-One and Cross-Functional Rings)

Cascade #4: Enterprise-Wide Change Execution Vehicles–Process and
Project Teams (Between-Departments Ring)

Cascade #5: Performance Management and Rewards
(Both One-to-One and Self Rings)

(arrow label: ENTERPRISE-WIDE CASCADE)

THE PARTS MUST FIT
Success is not the result of one action, but many actions,
each bringing us closer to you goal.

Leadership for Life Academy

SENIOR LEADERSHIP OF THE ENTERPRISE

Responsibility: for *What* is Cascaded

Accountability: for *How* well the cascade works

plus

Accountability: for Business Excellence and Superior Results

1420 Monitor Road • San Diego • California • 92110-1545 • (619) 275-6528 • Fax (619) 275-0324

SECTION VII
ASSESS YOUR
ORGANIZATIONAL DESIGN AND STRUCTURE

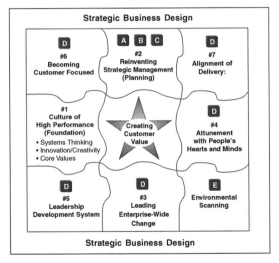

Strategic Business Design

"THE PARTS MUST FIT"

"Success is not the result of one action,
but many actions,
each bringing us closer to our goal."

Leadership for Life Academy

1420 Monitor Road • San Diego • California • 92110-1545 • (619) 275-6528 • Fax (619) 275-0324

THE TOP 10 FAILURES OF "FRAGMENTED FUNCTIONS" IN MOST ORGANIZATIONS

(vs. AN ORGANIZATION AS A LIVING SYSTEM)

1. Fragmented Information System

2. Fragmented Training and Development

3. Fragmented Department Goal Setting

4. Fragmented Unit Plans

5. Fragmented Measurements of Success

6. Fragmented Priorities/ Mind Maps

7. Fragmented Performance Appraisals

8. Fragmented Reward System

9. Fragmented Projects/ Consultants

10. Fragmented Leadership Development

Are We

Micro Start

and

Macro Dumb?

ebewc07.pmd

1420 Monitor Road • San Diego • California • 92110-1545 • (619) 275-6528 • Fax (619) 275-0324

—STRATEGIC MANAGEMENT ASSESSMENT—
THREE CORPORATE-WIDE CORE COMPETENCIES

Required of Every Successful Organization in the World

Keyword	Meaning	How to coordinate/ensure it succeeds
#1 **DEVELOP** **LEADERSHIP**	**Core Competency #1** *"DEVELOP & ACHIEVE LEADERSHIP EXCELLENCE"* Leadership Development System	Employee/Executive Development Board (plus Yearly Leadership Assessment)
#2 **PLANNING** **CYCLE**	**Core Competency #2** *"BUILD AN INTEGRATED STRATEGIC MANAGEMENT CYCLE"* Overall Strategic Management System	Planning/Strategic Change Steering Committee (plus Annual Strategic Review)
#3 **INTEGRATED** **CHANGE**	**Core Competency #3** *"CREATE A STRATEGIC BUSINESS DESIGN WITH WATERTIGHT INTEGRITY – TO YOUR VISION"* Integrated architecture of structures, processes, people, and systems to achieve Business Excellence	Strategy Sponsorship Teams, Innovation and Change Project Teams (plus *Building on Baldrige* Yearly Best Practices Assessment)

"Leading Enterprise-Wide Change"
Means
Leading the Development, Installation and Maintenance
of All Three Corporate-Wide Core Competencies
to Achieve Business Excellence.

ebewc07.pmd

1420 Monitor Road • San Diego • California • 92110-1545 • (619) 275-6528 • Fax (619) 275-0324

DATA-BASED DECISION-MAKING

1. What Data/Information do you have?
2. What do you need for better decision-making (i.e., more than just opinions, intuition and past experiences):

Topic	Data Available	Who Has It?	Data Needed	Who is Responsible?
I. Employees				
1. Satisfaction with Company Values				
2. Turnover				
3. Organization-Wide Assessment (Building on Baldrige)				
4. What Else?				
II. Customers				
5. Customer Satisfaction				
6. Customer Needs/Wants				
7. What Else?				
III. Marketing				
8. Market Segment Research				
9. Market Share Research				
10. Product Performance				
11. Competitor Analysis				
12. What Else?				
IV. Finance				
13. Balance Sheet				
14. P/L Statement				
15. ROE/ROA				
16. Cash Flow				
17. What Else?				

ebewc07.pmd

1420 Monitor Road • San Diego • California • 92110-1545 • (619) 275-6528 • Fax (619) 275-0324

SWOT FRAMEWORK

I. Internal to the Organization/Department (In Here)

Strengths — "Build On"	**W**eaknesses — "Eliminate/Cope"

II. External to the Organization/Department (in the Environment–Out There)

Opportunities— "Exploit"	**T**hreats — "Ease/Lower"

ORGANIZATION AS A SYSTEMS MODEL

ORGANIZATIONAL PIECES DEFINED:

What are the names of the parts/elements of any organization? List them — Brainstorm:

1.	16.
2.	17.
3.	18.
4.	19.
5.	20.
6.	21.
7.	22.
8.	23.
9.	24.
10.	25.
11.	26.
12.	27.
13.	28.
I4.	29.
15.	30.

ebewc07.pmd

1420 Monitor Road • San Diego • California • 92110-1545 • (619) 275-6528 • Fax (619) 275-0324

MACRO ISSUES WITH CHANGE

THE PARTS OF THE ORGANIZATION
DON'T FIT AND WORK TOGETHER

Marketing	PR	Finance
Manufacturing	Mission	Systems/Procedures
HR	Strategy	Tasks/Goals
DP	Values	Culture
Legal	Organization	Rewards/Feedback
Ops	Staffing	R&D

In Short...

the world can no longer be comprehended as a simple machine. It is a complex, highly interconnected system.

The Basic Trouble...

is that most people are still trying to solve the problems of a complex system with the mentality and tools that were appropriate for the world as a

Simple Machine

—Ian Mitroff

Mission ➔ Strategy ➔ Structure (or now "Strategic Business Design")

---

ebewc07.pmd

1420 Monitor Road • San Diego • California • 92110-1545 • (619) 275-6528 • Fax (619) 275-0324

THE INTERDEPENDENCE PARADIGM

*"We are all **interdependent** with each other."*

We all know that we are a part of a vast interrelated whole earth/universe—ever since the astronaut pictures of earth from space.

So why don't we focus on the interrelatedness of:

- our environment (everything outside of us)

- our relationships with all of our environment

- desired outcomes, visions, purposes

- sharing/agreeing on these visions

- gaining feedback on this vision and my part in it on a continuing and regular basis

---

Systems and Subsystems

—Dick Beckhard

A company is a system with many subsystems, all of which are interconnected.

Thinking in systems terms means being aware of the web of interrelationships that exist between the parts vs. being aware just of the parts themselves.

---

ebewc07.pmd

1420 Monitor Road • San Diego • California • 92110-1545 • (619) 275-6528 • Fax (619) 275-0324

THE FIT ISSUE

Excellence is doing 10,000 little things right (i.e., fitting them with 10,000 other little things) to achieve the desired culture.

The Key is follow through to ensure:

- adherence
- consistence

We Must be musicians who listen to the music; not just technicians.

The Key is to find out how to lock in the employees and customers emotionally:

- 15% of actions are rational/left brained
- 85% of actions are emotional/right brained

The Biggest Problem with "Fit" is the tendency for most things to immediately:

- fly apart again
- become technical vs. people oriented
- to put short term profits before long-term image and values

A Values Audit looks at the image and culture of the organization regarding perceptions vs. reality.

SYSTEMS THEORY EXAMPLES

- 1984 ESM securities dealer collapse
- October 19, 1987 stock market crash
- World's best car example
- Doctor's traditional injury treatment
- Ripple effect of a stone thrown into water
- Physical stress vs. emotions vs. illness
- Employee treatment vs. customer service

ebewc07.pmd

1420 Monitor Road • San Diego • California • 92110-1545 • (619) 275-6528 • Fax (619) 275-0324

ENTERPRISE-WIDE ASSESSMENT
through using THE BUSINESS EXCELLENCE ARCHITECTURE™

Name of Organization _____

Date _____

Instructions:

1. Please list each module's key strengths and weaknesses.
2. Then score each module (Put an X - Low 1 to 6 High).
3. Connect the scores with a straight line.

1. Building a Culture of Performance Excellence

2. Reinventing Strategic Planning

3. Leading Enterprise-Wide Change

4. Creating the People Edge

5. Achieving Leadership Excellence

6. Becoming Customer-Focused

7. Aligning Delivery

STRENGTHS

WEAKNESSES

HIGH 6 5 4 3 2 1 LOW

Assessment-1.eps

ebewc07.pmd

1420 Monitor Road • San Diego • California • 92110-1545 • (619) 275-6528 • Fax (619) 275-0324

ENTERPRISE-WIDE CHANGE IMPACT EXERCISE

CREATING A HIGH PERFORMANCE ORGANIZATION
(Using the A–B–C–D–E Phases and the "Business Excellence Architecture" Model)

What components of your organization will/should be impacted by the major change/strategy you propose? Which change/strategy?: _____

Which Components are Impacted and How?	Action Needed/Implications
Phase **E** **Environment** 1. _____ Environmental Scanning System 2. _____ Key Environmental Stakeholders (List): _____ _____	
Future Environmental Trends/Scan: 3. _____ S = Socio-demographics 4. _____ K = Competition 5. _____ E = Economics 6. _____ E = Natural Environment 7. _____ P = Political/Regulatory 8. _____ T = Technology 9. _____ I = Industry 10. _____ C = Customers	
Phase **A** **Module #8—Creating Customer Value (Quadruple Bottom Line):** 1. _____ Customer Satisfaction 2. _____ Employee Satisfaction 3. _____ Shareholder Satisfaction 4. _____ Community Satisfaction **Customer Positioning Choices:** 5. _____ Quality Services 6. _____ Quality Products 7. _____ Customer Service (Feelings) 8. _____ Customer Choices 9. _____ Lower Cost Products/Services 10. _____ Speed/Responsiveness/Convenience	

ebewc07.pmd

continued

1420 Monitor Road • San Diego • California • 92110-1545 • (619) 275-6528 • Fax (619) 275-0324

ENTERPRISE-WIDE CHANGE IMPACT EXERCISE

Which Components are Impacted and How?	Action Needed/Implications?
Module #2—Reinventing Strategic Planning: 1. _____ Vision 2. _____ Mission 3. _____ Organizational Values 4. _____ Organizational Positioning 5. _____ Organizational Identity/Image (Brand) 6. _____ Strategic Business Units 7. _____ Annual Operating Priorities 8. _____ Annual Department Plans 9. _____ Operating Budgets 10. _____ Capital Budgets 11. _____ Financing/Banks/Investors 12. _____ Annual Strategic Review (& Update)	
Phase B 13. _____ Key Success Measures— Outcome Measures (List): _____ _____ _____ 14. _____ Cascade of metrics to all Management levels	
Phase C 15. _____ Other Core Strategies (List): _____ _____ _____ _____ _____	

ebewc07.pmd

1420 Monitor Road • San Diego • California • 92110-1545 • (619) 275-6528 • Fax (619) 275-0324

ENTERPRISE-WIDE CHANGE IMPACT EXERCISE

Which Components are Impacted and How?	Action Needed/Implications?
Phase D	
Module #1—Culture of Performance Excellence: The Foundation:	
16. _____ Systems Thinking Language/Skills	
17. _____ Org'n as a Learning Org'n	
18. _____ Innovation & Creativity Language/ Skills	
19. _____ Adult Learning Theory (Experiential Learning)	
20. _____ Group Facilitation	
21. _____ Fact-based Decision-making	
Module #3—Leading Strategic Change:	
22. _____ Change Management Structures	
23. _____ Team Development	
24. _____ Strategic Business Design	
25. _____ Strategic Communication Processes	
26. _____ Empowerment	
27. _____ Key Internal Stakeholders (List): _____ _____ _____	
28. _____ Change Management Plans/ Processes	
Module #4—Attunement with People's Hearts:	
29. _____ Job Design/Definition	
30. _____ Staffing Levels (Recruitment/ Downsizing/Selection)	
31. _____ Performance Appraisal	
32. _____ Rewards System (Pay/Non-Pay)	

ebewc07.pmd

1420 Monitor Road • San Diego • California • 92110-1545 • (619) 275-6528 • Fax (619) 275-0324

ENTERPRISE-WIDE CHANGE IMPACT EXERCISE

Which Components are Impacted and How?	Action Needed/Implications?
Module #5—Leadership Development System:	
32. _____ Succession Planning for Executives & Management	
33. _____ Succession Planning for Key Other Jobs/Roles	
34. _____ Leadership Development System	
Training & Development:	
35. _____ Executives	
36. _____ Management/Supervisors	
37. _____ Sales & Marketing	
38. _____ Workforce Training	
Module #6—Becoming Customer Focused:	
39. _____ Strategic Marketing/Sales Planning	
40. _____ Market Research/Customer Needs	
41. _____ Sales Management	
42. _____ Marketing Management	
Module #7: Alignment of Delivery:	
43. _____ Daily Operating Tasks	
44. _____ Continuous Process Improvement/ Waste Elimination	
45. _____ Business Processes Re-engineered	
46. _____ Simplify Policies & Procedures	
47. _____ Enterprise-Wide Technology	
48. _____ Supply-Chain Management	
49. _____ Facilities & Equipment	
50. _____ Cross-Department Knowledge Transfer	

ebewc07.pmd

1420 Monitor Road • San Diego • California • 92110-1545 • (619) 275-6528 • Fax (619) 275-0324

WHAT'S THE USE OF THE
BUSINESS EXCELLENCE ARCHITECTURE MODEL?

1. A template, model, or diagnostic tool.
2. A framework for thinking and analyzing our organization (or department).
3. Questions to ask as I/we make decisions to change items/tasks in the organization (i.e., implement our Strategic Plan).
4. A common framework for thinking, communicating, and working together to change parts of our organization and achieve our Vision.
5. An increased awareness, sensitivity, and understanding of how an organization works and how the parts should fit together in support of our Vision/customers.
6. A tool to diagnose the status of our effectiveness in both achieving our organization's "fit, alignment, and integrity" to our vision and to our desired culture.
7. Exquisite simplicity, macro model; use it to get a handle on organizational changes.
8. To eliminate biases.
9. To give you a focus through organizational complexity.
10. Bird's eye view/framework to look at the overall organization.
    - multiple cause and effect
    - a balanced way to cover the waterfront
11. Help narrow in on areas needing work.
    - set priorities for work
    - clear linkages/interdependence to other functions, tasks
12. Road map—not get lost in the organization complexity.
    - know where you are and how to navigate to success
    - 21st century road map vs. 1700s map
13. Diagnose problems/solutions in organizations and how one thing affects all others to increase chance of success.
14. To explain, teach executives/managers how to manage/lead strategic planning/strategic change.
    - readiness check
15. A way to guide any large scale change and to improve individual/team performance and links to the vision/values, direction.
16. To have more confidence in your implementation.
17. To learn how multi-causes have multi-effects.
    - simple cause/effect is obsolete
18. Help ensure strategies/actions are based on a systems diagnosis.

> Complex systems are changed
> by small interventions
> (if in the right place)

ebewc07.pmd

1420 Monitor Road • San Diego • California • 92110-1545 • (619) 275-6528 • Fax (619) 275-0324

A TOTALLY INTEGRATED SYSTEMS SOLUTION

Centre Interventions:
Seamless and synergistic for ease of learning and doing

We provide 80% of the external consulting and training needs of most organizations – using our copyrighted Systems Thinking ApproachTM (the natural way the world works)

This use of only one mental or mind map and framework for thinking of **"your organization as a living system"** prevents the 75% failure rate experts agree happens to most major Strategic Planning and Enterprise-Wide Change efforts.

Our research has shown there are the **Big Three Failures** as a result of multiple mind maps:

#1   Analytic and piecemeal approaches to a System's Problem

#2   Mainly focusing on Economic Alignment of Delivery

#3   Mainly focusing on Cultural Attunement and Involvement with People

We can meet 80% of your needs.

If we cannot meet the other 20%, we will be the first to let you know.
Our integrity requires it.

THE YIN AND YANG OF STRATEGIES
(Positioning for a Competitive Edge and Customer Value)

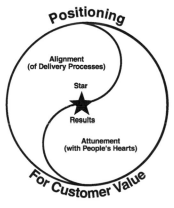

ebewc07.pmd

1420 Monitor Road • San Diego • California • 92110-1545 • (619) 275-6528 • Fax (619) 275-0324

GOAL #2

SECTION VIII
PROVIDE SIMPLICITY OF EXECUTION

IN A COMPLEX WORLD AND CHANGE PROCESS

"Enterprise-Wide Change is Like Riding a Bucking Bronco"

—unpleasant and unexpected events
—lots of violent ups and downs
—hard to hang on

—Steve Haines 11/24/01

ebewc08.pmd

1420 Monitor Road • San Diego • California • 92110-1545 • (619) 275-6528 • Fax (619) 275-0324

SIMPLICITY OF EXECUTION

Activity #1   Enterprise-Wide Change Leadership Team meets and develops the initial set of Core Strategies. (If not already in place.)

Activity #2   Large Group Parallel Involvement Process held as appropriate. To preserve the CEO and senior executive prerogative, we recommend this process only develop an initial Draft of the three to five Enterprise-Wide Key Initiatives under each Shared Core Strategy.

Activity #3   Final review and clean up of these initiatives by senior management.

Activity #4   Business Units, Divisions, and Major Departments adopt these Shared Core Strategies as their Department Goals for the next year. Then, they are ready to develop unit/departmental "Work Plans" to support these Strategies and Initiatives.

Activity #5   After these Unit Work Plans are developed, share them with the same group of people in the Large Group session of Activity #2.

Activity #6   The Change Leadership Team meets to format Innovative Process and Project Teams. They lead the execution of the Shared Core Strategies and Key Initiatives across functions to serve the Customer better (and achieve superior results).

Activity #7   Tie all rewards systems.

ebewc08.pmd

1420 Monitor Road • San Diego • California • 92110-1545 • (619) 275-6528 • Fax (619) 275-0324

KEYS TO SIMPLICITY OF EXECUTION— CASCADING SUBSYSTEMS:

WAVE AFTER WAVE OF CHANGES

Key #1 Regular meetings of the Change Leadership Team.

Key #2 Regular tracking and reporting about results achieved and measures of success.

Key #3 Change Consultants (internal/external) provide full time leadership from Program Management Office. Someone must be guiding the Enterprise-Wide Change journey on a daily basis.

Key #4 Concurrent development of the Enterprise-Wide Change **capacity and content** in five key change areas:
- Commitment capabilities
- Process
- Structures
- Competencies
- Resources

SIX BELIEFS DURING THE WAVES OF CHANGE

Belief #1: Enterprise-Wide Change is a constantly unfolding, discovery, creation, and recreation process that cascades through and across the organization.

Belief #2: The Systems Thinking Approach to living systems tells us that each "wave" of subsystem change must be planned, discussed, led, and implemented in relationship to other subsystems.

Belief #3: Each of these subsystems (and the people in them) go through the predictable six stages of the Rollercoaster of Change at different depths and rates.

Belief #4: The Systems Thinking Approach can and should be bolstered by traditional OD interventions, but these must always be linked to the larger purposes— Enterprise-Wide Change.

Belief #6: The ABC's simplicity framework of the Systems Thinking Approach™ has virtually unlimited uses in the waves of change—including all the traditional OD inventions.

Belief #5: The Program Management Office should lead these activities on a day-to-day basis to keep Failure #1 (Multiple Conflicting Mental Maps) from rearing its ugly head.

ebewc08.pmd

1420 Monitor Road • San Diego • California • 92110-1545 • (619) 275-6528 • Fax (619) 275-0324

WAVES OF CHANGE

SEVEN LEVELS OF LIVING (OPEN) SYSTEMS

1. Cell

2. Organ

3. Organism/Individual

4. Group   Organizational Focus

5. Organization

6. Society/Nation

7. Supranational System/Earth

Source: Kenneth Boulding

STRATEGIC CHANGE:
"SEVEN RINGS OF REALITY"

(Taken from "7 Levels of Living Systems")

- Increased complexity
- Readiness/willingness
- Skills growth

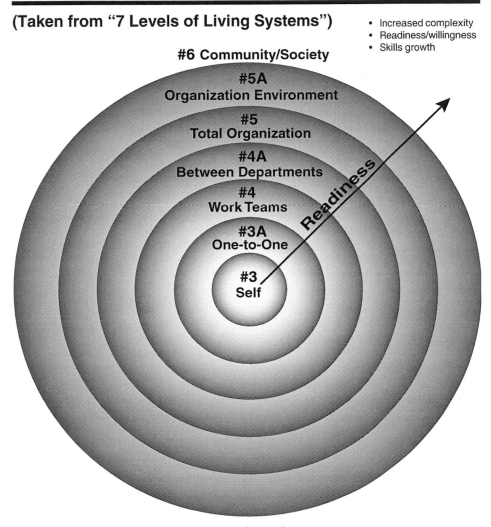

#6 Community/Society

#5A
Organization Environment

#5
Total Organization

#4A
Between Departments

#4
Work Teams

#3A
One-to-One

#3
Self

Readiness

Note: Rings 3–4–5 are 3 of the "7 Levels of Living Systems"
Rings 3A–4A–5A are "Collisions of Systems" interacting with other systems

Source: Stephen G. Haines, 1980; updated 1988, 1994, and 2003

ebewc08.pmd

1420 Monitor Road • San Diego • California • 92110-1545 • (619) 275-6528 • Fax (619) 275-0324

GENERAL PURPOSES OF WORKING AT EACH RING

"Seven Natural Rings of Reality"

Effectiveness (H–M–L):

Ring #3:   **Individuals ("Self-Mastery")**
_____
- Improve personal competency and effectiveness.
- Trustworthiness issues.

Ring #3A: **One-to-One Relationships ("Interpersonal Skills/Effectiveness")**
_____
- Improve the interpersonal and working relationships and effectiveness of each individual.
- Trust issues.

Ring #4:   **Workteams/Groups ("Team Empowerment/Effectiveness")**
_____
- Improve the effectiveness of the workteam as well as its members.
- Empowerment issues.

Ring #4A: **Intergroups ("Conflict/Horizontal Collaboration")**
_____
- Improve the working relationships and business processes between teams/departments horizontally to serve the customer better.
- Horizontal collaboration/integration issues.

Ring #5:   **Total Organization ("Fit"/Strategic Plan)**
_____
- Improve the organization's systems, structures and processes to better achieve its business results and potential; and develop its capacity to provide an adaptive system of change and response to a changing environment while pursuing your vision and strategic plan.
- Alignment issues.

Ring #5A: **Organization-Environment (Alliances)**
_____
- Improve the organization's sense of direction, response to Its' customers and proactive management of its environments/stakeholders by Reinventing Strategic Planning for the 21st Century (Includes Goal #1: Plans; Goal #2: Successful Implementation; and Goal #3: Sustaining Performance).
- Adaptation to the environment issues.

Ring #6:   **Community/Society**
- Improve the community's quality of life and its sense of health, well-being, safety, and prosperity.
- Any of the big or small diverse societal issues that exist, among cultures, special interests, professions, languages, neighborhoods, etc.

Source: Stephen G. Haines, 2/80; updated 3/88, 7/94, 1/03, and 2/04

ebewc08.pmd

1420 Monitor Road • San Diego • California • 92110-1545 • (619) 275-6528 • Fax (619) 275-0324

"SEVEN RINGS OF REALITY"

Seven Rings	Effectiveness (H–M–L)	Fit & Integration to Overall Vision
3. Individuals		
3A. One-to-One Relationships		
4. Workteams/Groups		
4A. Intergroups		
5. Total Organization		
5A. Organization-Environment		
6. Community/Society		

ebewc08.pmd

1420 Monitor Road • San Diego • California • 92110-1545 • (619) 275-6528 • Fax (619) 275-0324

INDIVIDUAL CHANGE

Individual change is hard —

Changing one's habits

is like writing your name in the snow,

in a snowstorm.

Many researchers believe it takes

18-24 months for a person to change their habits

— the ruts in the road that help and hinder us.

SUCCESSFUL INDIVIDUAL CHANGE

Do they have the Knowledge, Skills, Attitude?

K	=	IU	=	Intellectual Understanding
S	=	AI	=	Through Active Involvement/Participation
A	=	ES	=	Emotional Support by Others

and

Can they identify WIIFM?

1420 Monitor Road • San Diego • California • 92110-1545 • (619) 275-6528 • Fax (619) 275-0324

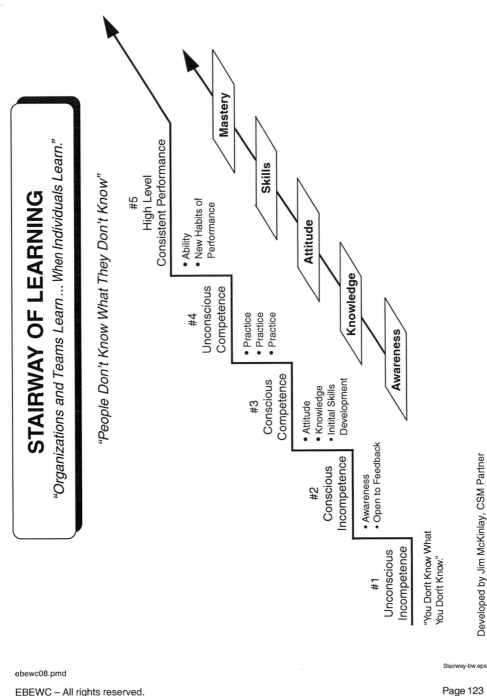

STAIRWAY OF LEARNING

"Organizations and Teams Learn ... When Individuals Learn."

"People Don't Know What They Don't Know"

#1
Unconscious
Incompetence

"You Don't Know What You Don't Know."

#2
Conscious
Incompetence
- Awareness
- Open to Feedback

#3
Conscious
Competence
- Attitude
- Knowledge
- Initital Skills Development

#4
Unconscious
Competence
- Practice
- Practice
- Practice

#5
High Level
Consistent Performance
- Ability
- New Habits of Performance

Awareness

Knowledge

Attitude

Skills

Mastery

Developed by Jim McKinlay, CSM Partner

Stairway-bw.eps

ebewc08.pmd

1420 Monitor Road • San Diego • California • 92110-1545 • (619) 275-6528 • Fax (619) 275-0324

TEAMS AS IMPLEMENTATION VEHICLES

The Flow

1. Groups are not teams.

2. Teams are structures.

3. Structures influences behaviors.

4. Are their behaviors team oriented?

5. Do you Team-oriented Members know how to run project teams?

The Question:

When does a group

become

an effective team?

1420 Monitor Road • San Diego • California • 92110-1545 • (619) 275-6528 • Fax (619) 275-0324

EFFECTIVE TEAM FUNCTIONING

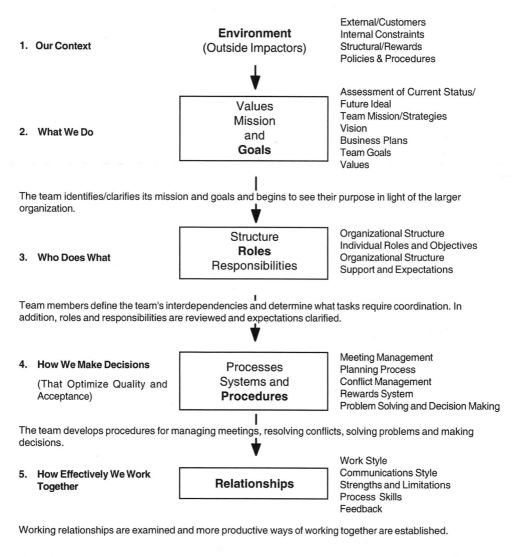

1. Our Context

Environment
(Outside Impactors)

External/Customers
Internal Constraints
Structural/Rewards
Policies & Procedures

2. What We Do

Values
Mission
and
Goals

Assessment of Current Status/
Future Ideal
Team Mission/Strategies
Vision
Business Plans
Team Goals
Values

The team identifies/clarifies its mission and goals and begins to see their purpose in light of the larger organization.

3. Who Does What

Structure
Roles
Responsibilities

Organizational Structure
Individual Roles and Objectives
Organizational Structure
Support and Expectations

Team members define the team's interdependencies and determine what tasks require coordination. In addition, roles and responsibilities are reviewed and expectations clarified.

4. How We Make Decisions

(That Optimize Quality and Acceptance)

Processes
Systems and
Procedures

Meeting Management
Planning Process
Conflict Management
Rewards System
Problem Solving and Decision Making

The team develops procedures for managing meetings, resolving conflicts, solving problems and making decisions.

5. How Effectively We Work Together

Relationships

Work Style
Communications Style
Strengths and Limitations
Process Skills
Feedback

Working relationships are examined and more productive ways of working together are established.

ebewc08.pmd

1420 Monitor Road • San Diego • California • 92110-1545 • (619) 275-6528 • Fax (619) 275-0324

INNOVATIVE PROJECT TEAMS
(The Vehicle for Execution of Enterprise-Wide Change)

EXERCISE: Think of a Project Team You Were Recently On:_____

LIST HERE

Project Teams Require Unique Skills to Function Effectively.

These Needed Skills Include:	Level of Performance Low ├─┼─┼─┤ High 1 2 3 4 5	Comments:
1. Effective Teamwork	├─┼─┼─┼─┤	
2. Innovation	├─┼─┼─┼─┤	
3. Project Management	├─┼─┼─┼─┤	
4. Systems Thinking	├─┼─┼─┼─┤	
5. Clarity of Purposes	├─┼─┼─┼─┤	
6. Simplicity of Execution	├─┼─┼─┼─┤	
7. Rollercoaster of Change	├─┼─┼─┼─┤	
8. Facilitating Conflict	├─┼─┼─┼─┤	

What Actions Are Needed?	To Do List	By Whom	By When

ebewc08.pmd

1420 Monitor Road • San Diego • California • 92110-1545 • (619) 275-6528 • Fax (619) 275-0324

CASCADE OF CHANGE

STRATEGIC MANAGEMENT REALITY CHECK

Talk is cheap. That's apparent from the results of a survey of more than 500 small and midsize companies conducted by the Oechsli Institute. Many of their employees say management's actions don't support the mission statement and that their company's workers don't understand what's expected of them. Worse, 8 out of 10 managers, salespeople, and operations employees say they are not held accountable for their own daily performance.

Percentage that answered yes among. . .	Management	Sales/frontline employees
Does your company have a clear written mission statement? ↓	97%	77%
Is that statement supported by management's actions? ↓	54%	55%
Do all departments, branches, and divisions have specific and measurable goals? ↓	54%	57%
Does every employee understand what is expected in terms of performance? ↓	46%	38%
Are all employees held accountable for daily performance?	21%	22%

Source: Performance Survey, the Oechsli Institute, Greensboro, NC; Reprinted in INC./March 1993.
Research repeated by DDI, Training Magazine, June 2003 (with substantially the same results).

ebewc08.pmd

THE CASCADE OF CHANGE
The Systems Thinking Approach™

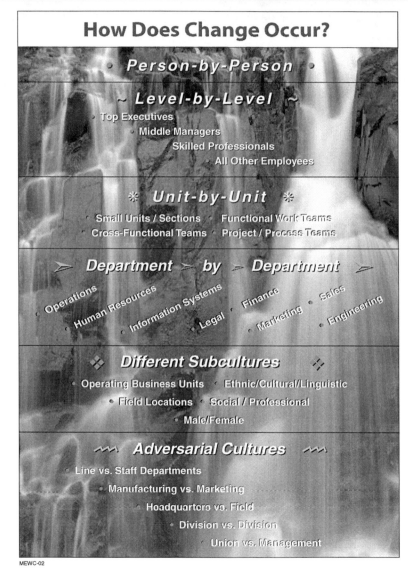

How Does Change Occur?

Person-by-Person

~ Level-by-Level ~
- Top Executives
- Middle Managers
- Skilled Professionals
- All Other Employees

✳ Unit-by-Unit ✳
- Small Units / Sections · Functional Work Teams
- Cross-Functional Teams · Project / Process Teams

Department ➤ by ➤ Department
Operations · Human Resources · Information Systems · Legal · Finance · Marketing · Sales · Engineering

❖ Different Subcultures ❖
- Operating Business Units · Ethnic/Cultural/Linguistic
- Field Locations · Social / Professional
- Male/Female

〰 Adversarial Cultures 〰
- Line vs. Staff Departments
- Manufacturing vs. Marketing
- Headquarters vs. Field
- Division vs. Division
- Union vs. Management

MEWC-02

ebewc08.pmd

1420 Monitor Road • San Diego • California • 92110-1545 • (619) 275-6528 • Fax (619) 275-0324

CASCADE OF CHANGE – EXERCISE

What different cultures do you have in your organization?

1.   Person-by-Person:

2.   Level-by-Level:

3.   Unit-by-Unit:

4.   Department-by-Department:

5.   Different Subcultures:

6.   Adversarial Cultures:

Total # of different cultures = _____

CASCADE #2: BUSINESS UNIT AND STAFF LEADERSHIP

FIRST:

> **BUSINESS UNIT AND STAFF 3-YEAR BUSINESS PLANS**
> (Work *ON* the Sub-System)

THEN:

> **CASCADE #2: BUSINESS/STAFF UNITS**
> (Work *IN* the Sub-System)

Cascade the Enterprise-Wide Change Journey throughout each Business Unit and Staff Function:

Cascade #1: Shared Core Enterprise-Wide Change Strategies – may be tailored
(Total-Sub-System Ring)

Cascade #2: Large Group Enterprise-Wide 3-Year Plan Reviews
(One-to-One/Cross-Functional Rings)

Cascade #3: Unit/Department/Section Annual Plans
(Work-Teams Ring)

Cascade #4: Execution Vehicles–Lead some Process and Project Teams
and Support Others (Cross-Departments Ring)

Cascade #5: Performance Management and Rewards
(Both One-to-One and Self Rings)

(diagonal text along arrow: BUSINESS/STAFF UNIT CASCADE)

THE PARTS MUST FIT
Success is not the result of one action, but many actions,
each bringing us closer to you goal.

Leadership for Life Academy

BUSINESS UNIT/STAFF SENIOR LEADERSHIP

Responsibility: for *What* is Cascaded

Accountability: for *How well* the cascade works

plus

Accountability: for Business Excellence and Superior Results
(for your area of responsibility)

ebewc08.pmd

1420 Monitor Road • San Diego • California • 92110-1545 • (619) 275-6528 • Fax (619) 275-0324

ENTERPRISE-WIDE CULTURAL CHANGE

Enterprise-Wide Change

Always

Involves Cultural Change

When Culture and Strategy Collide

Which Wins Out?

Culture, Of Course

IMPORTANCE OF ORGANIZATIONAL CULTURE

As companies move from hierarchical, top-down organizations, a greater number of the decisions individuals make are shaped by the firm's culture

—*Personnel Journal*

Organizational culture can create an environment that helps, hinders, or confuses the achievement of organizational goals. Without careful attention to the impact change has on all aspects of an organization, the drive for competitive advantage can be thwarted by a non-supportive cultural environment.

—Thomas K. Theodore and Lou Bronson
Management Review

ebewc08.pmd

1420 Monitor Road • San Diego • California • 92110-1545 • (619) 275-6528 • Fax (619) 275-0324

ORGANIZATIONAL CULTURE DEFINED

THE WAY WE DO BUSINESS AROUND HERE

Organizational culture is a set of interrelated beliefs or norms shared by most of the employees of an organization about how one should behave at work and what activities are more important than others.

Assumptions/Philosophy =
Our World View
("Weltanschauung")

$\vee$

Personal Values

$\vee$

Organizational Values

$\vee$

Norms of Behavior
(i.e., the standards for action)

$\vee$

Individual Behavior

**Collectively
Leads to Our
Culture**

*(This topic requires its own Executive Briefing
Initiative – as it is that difficult and important)*

ebewc08.pmd

1420 Monitor Road • San Diego • California • 92110-1545 • (619) 275-6528 • Fax (619) 275-0324

LENGTH OF TIME TO CHANGE AN ORGANIZATION

(From Start to Finish vs. the "Quick Fix")

1.   To build a new plant or headquarters building.

2.   To acquire/develop a new drug, obtain regulatory approval, and assimilate it into/out of our firm's marketing effort..

3.   To make a "best selling" new product/book.

4.   To explore for, refine, and pump the oil into my car's gas tank.

5.   To develop a new, higher capacity computer chip.

6.   To build a new type of airliner.

7.   To change a total organization's direction, culture and employee motivation in support of this change.

> Think Long-Term
> *and*
> Short-Term

"Think downboard" as they do in chess!

How Long Does Culture Change Take?

ebewc08.pmd

1420 Monitor Road • San Diego • California • 92110-1545 • (619) 275-6528 • Fax (619) 275-0324

HOW DO YOU CREATE A LEARNING ORGANIZATION

Question: What are our needed actions to create a learning organization? (H–M–L) Use all Seven Tracks to a High Performance Organization as places where learning needs to occur (i.e., executive leadership, teams, management skills, etc.)

_____ 1. Reward managers who try to create it.

_____ 2. Process meetings at the end to improve them.

_____ 3. Conduct training and learning experiences at each staff meeting.

_____ 4. Create "whole jobs" with direct customer contact. Give people the autonomy and freedom to act/control their own jobs ("Every Employee a Manager").

_____ 5. Provide jobs/tasks to everyone that include OJT and new learning experiences.

_____ 6. Conduct training — training — training with follow-up and applications review so it is meaningful/useful to people's jobs.

_____ 7. Understand and use "adult learning theory" as a way to present any/all new situations. Supply people with questions, not solutions.

_____ 8. Set up a "52-week" training program (bite-sized learning).

_____ 9. Set up periodic and regular personal feedback to employees on how they come across to others and on their job performance vs. objectives.

_____ 10. Set up a complete, strategic, and all management levels Management Development System. Use managers/executives as the trainers to help them learn better.

_____ 11. Train and evaluate managers and executives in their new role of the 1990s (i.e., TLC — trainer, leader, coach).

_____ 12. Work on continuous performance improvement and delegation daily. Track it.

_____ 13. Set up debriefings and "post mortums" to ensure we learn from our mistakes and experiences.

_____ 14. Help the organization and culture develop a "forgiveness and problem-solving vs. blaming" culture. Promote experimentation, discovery, and mistake making as a way to learn.

_____ 15. Inspire a shared vision/common purpose that people can relate to and enthusiastically embrace.

_____ 16. What else?

> A learning organization is an organization skilled at creating, acquiring, and transferring knowledge, and at modifying its behavior to reflect new knowledge and insights.
>
> —*Harvard Business Review*
> July-August 1993

ebewc08.pmd

1420 Monitor Road • San Diego • California • 92110-1545 • (619) 275-6528 • Fax (619) 275-0324

LEVELS OF THE LEARNING ORGANIZATION

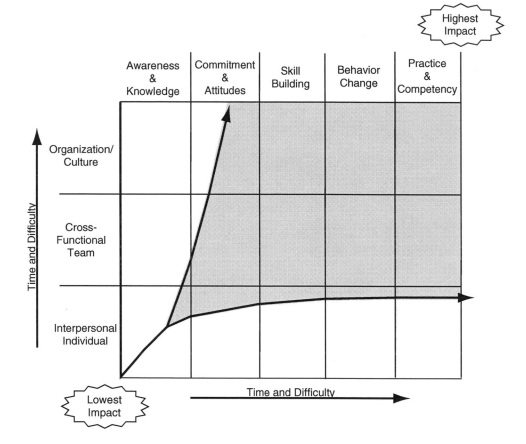

1420 Monitor Road • San Diego • California • 92110-1545 • (619) 275-6528 • Fax (619) 275-0324

ENTERPRISE-WIDE CHANGE

GOING TO SCALE vs. "TOO LOW A DOSAGE"

The Real Issue:

The real issue is not

a pilot project or continuous improvement

but

can we ever "go to scale"?

Usually, we provide too low a dosage

to have a big impact.

• Do we know what this means?

• How do you do it?

Enterprise-Wide Change:
Courage & Stamina

"The problem...is not that the change has not started, but that is simmers along, **never quite reaching a boil**. It simmers because we often fail to realize that being world-class requires a long-term commitment to transforming the workplace....

Change also simmers because people at all levels often do not have the courage and stamina they need to carry them through the inevitable dark hours of resistance and confusion that accompany fundamental change.

—*Patricia McLagan and Christo Nel*

Source: "The Age of Participation", Training & Development, March 1996

ebewc08.pmd

1420 Monitor Road • San Diego • California • 92110-1545 • (619) 275-6528 • Fax (619) 275-0324

ENTERPRISE-WIDE CHANGE

THREE LEVELS OF THE CASCADE OF CHANGE...

(and the Central Importance of Leadership/Management Skills and Structure)

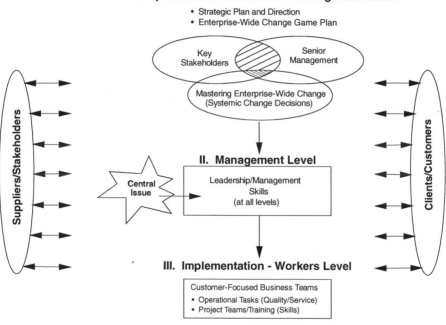

I. Sponsors/Leaders/CEO/Sr. Management Level
- Strategic Plan and Direction
- Enterprise-Wide Change Game Plan

Key Stakeholders

Senior Management

Mastering Enterprise-Wide Change
(Systemic Change Decisions)

Suppliers/Stakeholders

Clients/Customers

II. Management Level
Leadership/Management
Skills
(at all levels)

Central Issue

III. Implementation - Workers Level
Customer-Focused Business Teams
- Operational Tasks (Quality/Service)
- Project Teams/Training (Skills)

Foundation Level – Capacity

1. **Commitment:**	• Commitment of Leaders of an Organization to Culture Change
2. **Process:**	• Dealing With Suppliers and Customers • The HR, Administrative, and Rewards System
3. **Structure:**	• Enterprise-Wide Change Management System • Organization Design – Business Excellence Architecture
4. **Capabilities:**	• Six Levels of Leadership Competencies • Enterprise-Wide Change Competencies
5. **Resources:**	• Adequate Resources for the Change

Three Levels.eps

ebewc08.pmd

1420 Monitor Road • San Diego • California • 92110-1545 • (619) 275-6528 • Fax (619) 275-0324

GOAL #3

SECTION IX
SUSTAIN A SYSTEM OF SUPERIOR RESULTS YEAR AFTER YEAR

"Permanence, perseverance, and persistence in spite of all obstacles, discouragements, and possibilities:

It is this that in all things distinguishes the strong soul from the weak."

—*Thomas Carlyle*

When you're finished changing, you're finished.

—*Benjamin Franklin*

B

Measures
Feedback

ebewc09.pmd

1420 Monitor Road • San Diego • California • 92110-1545 • (619) 275-6528 • Fax (619) 275-0324

BOOSTER SHOTS & FEEDBACK

DEFINITIONS:

SYN-ER-GY: Must be fostered

- The working together of two or more parts of any system, to produce an effect greater than the sum of the individual effects.

- Increasing the outcome by working together in a particularly effective way.

EN-TRO-PY: Must be reversed

- A measure of the amount of energy unavailable for work on a system.

- A tendency for any system to run down and eventually become inert.

Booster Rockets
"Booster Shots" are required for the
Space Shuttle to reach orbit.

1420 Monitor Road • San Diego • California • 92110-1545 • (619) 275-6528 • Fax (619) 275-0324

SIGNS OF ORGANIZATIONAL ENTROPY

Entropy

All business problems conform to the laws of inertia
—the longer you wait,
the harder the problem is to correct.

Incremental Degradation...

is the main barrier to achieving
the "fit" of all organization processes and actions
with the
espoused corporate values/vision.

From: *New Management* by Max DePree, CEO, Herman Miller

- A tendency toward superficiality.
- A dark tension among key people.
- No longer have time for celebration and ritual.
- A recurring effort by some to convince others that business is, after all, quite simple. (The acceptance of complexity and ambiguity and the ability to deal with them constructively is essential.)
- When problem-makers outnumber problem-solvers.
- When folks confuse heroes with celebrities.
- When leaders seek to control rather than liberate.
- When the pressure of day-to-day operations pushes aside our concern for vision and risk.
- An orientation toward the dry rules of business school rather than a value orientation which takes into account such things as contribution, spirit, excellence, beauty, and joy.
- When people speak of customers as impositions on their time rather than as opportunities to serve.
- When manuals grow in size.
- When leaders rely on structures instead of people.
- When a loss of grace and style and civility occurs.
- When a loss of respect for the English language occurs.

ebewc09.pmd

BUSINESS "SURVIVAL SKILL"

"FEEDBACK IS THE BREAKFAST OF CHAMPIONS"

Feedback is a gift; allow others to give it to you!

Question: Where do you get "feedback" today?

- It is the skill of being open and receptive to ... and even encouraging feedback from:
  - _____ all your customers
  - _____ all your employees
  - _____ all your direct reports and peers
  - _____ and anyone who can help you to learn and grow, as a person and human being, as a professional, as a leader of your organization

- Why is this important?

- How do you develop self-mastery (i.e., the external *style* and *inner psyche* to genuinely encourage others to help you with this *gift* of feedback, even when it *hurts)?*

Reinforcement/Feedback Systems To Sustain New Behaviors

ebewc09.pmd

1420 Monitor Road • San Diego • California • 92110-1545 • (619) 275-6528 • Fax (619) 275-0324

CONSENSUS ON FEEDBACK

1. "Feedback is the breakfast of champions."

2. Feedback is descriptive, not evaluation (if possible).

3. Even constructive feedback can be painful.
   "Growth is painful."

4. Am I expanding my range of information about myself?
   – *or* – Am I defending myself and my ego (and limiting my feedback)?–i.e.
   > *Do I want to be right or effective?*
   > *Which is it?*

5. So, are we willing to talk about the "pink elephant" in the middle of the room?–i.e.
   > *"Be honest and straight forward."*

6. If we "value" feedback, then it guides our behavior by processing each session at the end and giving each of us feedback.–i.e.

   1. Have an observer for our meeting/or each person assigned to observe another, or have "Feedback Roll-Up" sheets for us to give everyone feedback:

      - What did "X" do well today?

      - Where could "X" improve their interpersonal/team skills based on today's behavior?

Practice and Feedback

For decades, great athletic teams have harbored one simple secret that only a few select business teams have discovered, and it is this: to play and win together, you must practice together.

—Lewis Edwards

(and get brutally honest feedback on your practice/performance)

—Stephen Haines

---

ebewc09.pmd

1420 Monitor Road • San Diego • California • 92110-1545 • (619) 275-6528 • Fax (619) 275-0324

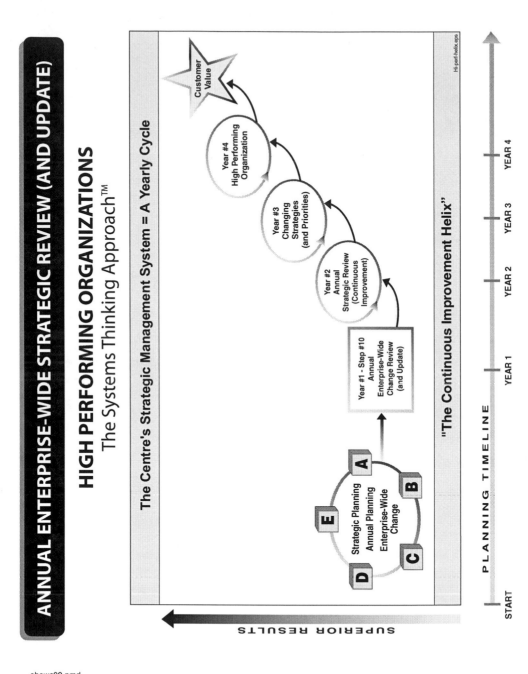

ANNUAL ENTERPRISE-WIDE STRATEGIC REVIEW (AND UPDATE)

HIGH PERFORMING ORGANIZATIONS
The Systems Thinking Approach™

The Centre's Strategic Management System = A Yearly Cycle

Customer Value

Year #4
High Performing Organization

Year #3
Changing Strategies
(and Priorities)

Year #2
Annual Strategic Review
(Continuous Improvement)

Year #1 - Step #10
Annual Enterprise-Wide Change Review (and Update)

Strategic Planning
Annual Planning
Enterprise-Wide Change

A B C D E

"The Continuous Improvement Helix"

PLANNING TIMELINE

START YEAR 1 YEAR 2 YEAR 3 YEAR 4

SUPERIOR RESULTS

Hi-perf-helix.eps

ebewc09.pmd

Page 144

ANNUAL ENTERPRISE-WIDE CHANGE REVIEW AND UPDATE

Activity #1: Two-day (or more) Annual Enterprise-Wide Change Review offsite meeting with Senior Management and key others.

Activity #2: Another participative plan to involve the entire organization in helping to plan the new Key Initiatives.

Activity #3: Second offsite meeting by Senior Management to review and finalize the revised game plan.

Activity #4: Development of new unit—division—department Work Plans based on these shared Core Strategies and Key Initiatives.

Activity #5: Large group Department Review to ensure continued commitment, and consensus about the Enterprise-Wide Change.

Activity #6: Leadership Teams continues regular meetings throughout the year.

Goal #3: Sustain a System of Results

Key actions include:

- Conducting a new future environmental scan (SKEPTIC).

- Reviewing and assessing the business results and the Quadruple Bottom Line results from the last year.

- Assessing yourself organization-wide vs. your mental model of an *organization as a system* (such as our Business Excellence Architecture).

- Assessing the results of the first year of the Enterprise-Wide Change Process itself.

- Assessing the results of the first year of your capacity to build and sustain the change.

- Assessing how well you are walking the talk on your core values. Then, developing further action plans to correct areas of weaknesses or failures.

- Redoing the Enterprise-Wide Change Game Plan for the next 12 months, adjusting Core Strategies, and Key Initiatives as necessary.

- Evaluating and redesigning the innovative project teams to ensure they continue to be effective vehicles for successful execution.

- Readjusting your Menu of Change Structures to ensure the proper infrastructure.

> ### Clarity and Simplicity are what's left over after everything else fails.
> *– Steve Haines*

ebewc09.pmd

1420 Monitor Road • San Diego • California • 92110-1545 • (619) 275-6528 • Fax (619) 275-0324

ANNUAL EWC STRATEGIC REVIEW

Annual Enterprise-Wide Change Strategic Review

"Similar to a yearly independent financial audit and update"

Goal #1: Assess the Strategic Management / EWC Process itself

Goal #2: Assess the status of the EWC Strategic Plan achievement itself

Goal #3: Assess your Enterprise-Wide Change Capacity Level

Resulting in:

1. Updating your EWC Game Plan/Strategic Plan

2. Clarifying your annual planning and EWC/strategic budgeting priorities for next year

3. Problem solving any issues raised in either goal

4. Setting in place next year's Annual Plan EWC Change Management Process, and Capacity-Building.

ebewc09.pmd

SECTION X
PUTTING IT ALL TOGETHER

CHANGE PROCESS PROTOTYPE – SUMMARY

Sequence

1. **Need for change.** (Mull it over; then go!)
2. Get "educated and organized" — **Smart Start** — formal or informal.
   Including:
   - Executive Briefing/Plan-to-Implement
   - Needed Organizational Assessments (Business Excellence Architecture)
   - Skill Building (Strategic Leadership Practices/Mastering Enterprise-Wide Change)
   - Set-up Change Leadership Team
   - Primary structures/roles set up—Especially Change Agent Cadre and Program Management Office
   - Process — change design principles — resources clear — capacity assessment
   - Match up process with ongoing events
3. Set in place the guiding structures/foundational capabilities and Yearly Comprehensive Map.
4. Clear direction — vision — charter — mental map of Systems Thinking = Game Plan.
5. Focus on the *Organization as a System* Model/mental map agreed to.
6. **Initial communications** — rollout — kickoff — stump speeches.
   - Unfreeze
   - Clear mental map
   - Vision – why?
   - Priority setting
7. Tie it to **Accountability Systems**:
   - Annual plans and budgets
   - Goal setting
   - Rewards/performance appraisals
   - Success measures/benchmarks
   - Customer research/needs/wants
8. Set up a **Leadership Development System** and Personal Leadership Plans; led by an Executive Development Board.
9. Focus on executive/middle management ownership; skill building on Enterprise-Wide Change management and Trainer–Coach–Facilitator/self mastery.
10. Audit Strategic HR Management Best Practices — redesign/conduct Strategic HR Planning.
11. Focus on **project team development** (Plan-Do-Control Cycle/skills):
    - Especially Executive Team Development
    - Especially cross-functional teamwork/team learning
12. Focus on business process reengineering — based on customer needs/wants/waste removal — Blow Out Bureaucracy – **Simplicity!**
    - Especially new teams
13. Spread implementation to full value-added delivery to the customer and full systemic redesign.
14. **Waterfall of Change** – Focus on all levels – individuals/teams, departments, entire organization/culture change.
15. Communicate – communicate – communicate (repetition).
16. Feedback – feedback – feedback ("is the breakfast of champions"): Learning!

ebewc10.pmd

1420 Monitor Road • San Diego • California • 92110-1545 • (619) 275-6528 • Fax (619) 275-0324

IMPLEMENTING ENTERPRISE-WIDE CHANGE

"TAILORED TO YOUR NEEDS"

Instructions: Please list the importance (H-M-L) to your Enterprise of adding and installing the following **Enterprise-Wide Change Management Processes** in order to achieve your Vision and Values. (i.e., What do you still need to do?)

Scoring Code: H = major need; **M** = smaller need or just refine existing skills processes or program; **L** = not applicable or already in place and functioning effectively.

Steps #1-5— Strategic Planning

_____ 1.   Environmental Scanning *System* in place?

_____ 2.   Key Success Factors with targets set and all tracking systems in place?

_____ 3.   Do you have clear data (i.e., Employee Survey) on your strengths and weaknesses in your Values and a specific action plan to eliminate these weaknesses within the next 1-2 years?

_____ 4.   Do you have a clear customer feedback and an ongoing system on your strengths and weaknesses vs. their expectations?

_____ 5.   Are realistic yearly organization-wide "must do" action priorities in place with lead accountability, time frames and resources allocated to them?

Step #6—Business Planning

_____ 6.   Do all business units have 3 year Business Plans in place?

_____ 7.   Do all major support departments have 3-Year Business Plans in place?

Step #7—Annual Plans, Budgets, and Accountability

_____ 8.   Does each major department have annual department Work Plans in place, using the organization's core strategies and annual action priorities?

_____ 9.   Have all major Department Plans been shared and critiqued with the Collective Management Team?

_____10.   Are all "must do" annual priorities funded?

_____11.   Do you have a clear and specific **Cascade of Accountability** for your desired outcomes, measures, and Core Strategy Achievement?

Step #8A—Smart Start and Plan-to-Implement

_____12.   Have you developed an Enterprise-Wide Change **"Game Plan"** and overall Change Process?

_____13.   Are all your needed Strategic Change Management Structures in place, based on all Structural Menu options?

_____14.   Do you specifically have in place a Change Leadership Team that meets every month?

continued

_____15. Have you installed an Executive/Employee Development Board (EDB), led personally by the CEO, to ensure that proper succession planning and people issues have a focal point?

_____16. Have you installed a Program Management Office (PMO) to guide, manage, coordinate, and integrate the day-to-day multiple set of Change Project Teams?

_____17. Do you have a Yearly Comprehensive Map of implementation in place, including when to conduct your Annual Strategic Review (and Strategic Plan Update)?

_____18. Has your Organization Design been redone to properly support the new direction?

_____19. Have you reviewed and developed a game plan to tailor and install the five basic elements of the needed Organizational Capacity as a foundation for sustaining the change?

_____20. Are the Change Principles clear and articulated to guide the entire change effort?

_____21. Are the Behavioral Science Principles clear and articulated to guide the entire change effort?

_____22. Do you have a *complete rollout plan* to get a simplified version (trifold, etc.) of your Strategic Plan to all employees and to have them understand it?

_____23. Do you have a plan to ensure building a critical mass for change, including individual transition support, entire organizational participation, Parallel Involvement Process, etc.?

Step #8B—Mastering Enterprise-Wide Change

_____24. Do you have the skills throughout your Collective Management Team to successfully lead and manage an Enterprise-Wide Change effort?

_____25. Has the **Rollercoaster of Change Best Practices Assessment** and Checklist been used to plan out the sequence and process the six stages of change (since it is natural, normal, and predictable)?

_____26. Do you have a specific **"Culture Change"** Game Plan and Project in place to start and change your culture directly?

Step #8C—Executive Development/Accountability

_____27. Do you have Personal Leadership Plans for all senior executives to show ongoing support for your Vision, Values and Strategies?

_____28. Do you have a Strategic Communications Plan to continually reinforce the desired changes again and again (repetition—4 times)?

_____29. Do you have a Leadership Development System in place to develop your collective leadership/management as a key to success?

_____30. Do you have a one-on-one coaching/mentoring process in place for your CEO and senior executives to continually support their growth and management of this change?

_____31. Does the senior management team need to be a more effective team?

_____32. Does the Collective Management Team need to improve their skills in conflict management?

ebewc10.pmd

continued

1420 Monitor Road • San Diego • California • 92110-1545 • (619) 275-6528 • Fax (619) 275-0324

Step #8D—Strategy Sponsorship Teams

33. List your **"Alignment of Delivery" strategies**. Have you conducted a "strategic impact exercise" for each and do you need Cross-Functional Project Teams for them in order to coordinate your organization's efforts?

Strategies	Impact Exercise	SST
1.		
2.		
3.		
4.		
5.		

34. List your **"Attunement With People's Hearts" strategies**. Have you conducted a "strategic impact exercise" for each and do you need Cross-Functional Project Teams in order to coordinate your organization's efforts?

Strategies	Impact Exercise	SST
1.		
2.		
3.		
4.		
5.		

Step #8E—Bureaucracy, Simplicity, and Funding

35. Do you need to get a fast start and grab people's attention to the change process (cut through and blow-out old bureaucracy)?

36. Will you have the money to fully fund a Strategic (Enterprise-Wide) Change Management Process?

37. Do you have a designated **"Simplicity Police"** (team, unit, committee) in place to build in *simplicity* as a competitive advantage (and huge cost savings)?

Step #8F—Change Cadre

38. Do you need internal change agent cadre (line and staff) skill development to support your change effort (including Subject Matter Experts (SMEs))?

Step #8G—Compatible Rewards Systems

39. Has your performance review/appraisal been redone and well communicated/understood to evaluate everyone on (1) adherence to Values, (2) strategic contribution and (3) learning/growth?

40. Do you have an organization-wide "Recognition of Results System" in place to support your Core Strategies and Values?

41. Have you revamped your financial incentive programs to support your Strategic Plan and Key Success Measures; including organization-wide and team rewards, as well as individual and department incentives?

ebewc10.pmd

continued

1420 Monitor Road • San Diego • California • 92110-1545 • (619) 275-6528 • Fax (619) 275-0324

Step #8H—Teams (not groups of individuals)

_____42. Does the organization have effective team and teamwork skills:

_____ a. within and/or

_____ b. across departments?

_____43. Do the Project Teams need more skills to become effective teams?

_____44. Are there other new teams that need effective team skills? List them:

_____ a.

_____ b.

_____ c.

45. Have the skills and tools of using Strategic and Systems Thinking on a daily basis been acquired by:

_____ a. the new teams and

_____ b. the Collective Management team?

_____46. Has the "Plan-Do-Control" task cycle been disseminated to the new teams and Collective Management Team to help in their work?

47. Have the many uses of the _Rollercoaster of Change_ been taught to:

_____ a. the new teams?

_____ b. the Collective Management Team to help in their work?

_____ c. all employees in advance of any change?

Step #9A—Enterprise-Wide Change Management Process

48. Have the following different employee transition needs been taken into consideration?

_____ a. Individual employee self mastery of change/interpersonal skills?

_____ b. Employee involvement, empowerment and accountability enhanced?

_____ c. Small unit leadership and participative management skills?

_____ d. Parallel Involvement Process and participation to accelerate the cultural change process?

49. Do you have adequate ongoing feedback/debriefing and learning mechanisms in place to assess, continuously improve, learn and sustain momentum?

_____ a. For executives?

_____ b. For teams?

_____ c. For projects?

_____ d. For meetings?

Step #9B—Cascade and Waves of Change

_____50. Has the needed cascade or waves of change (levels/units/employees) been identified and plans been developed to ensure success (including follow-up/booster shots)?

Step #9C—Alignment of Delivery

_____51. a. Do the organization's computer and telecommunications technology have a specific change game plan in place to support the Strategic Direction?

_____52. b. Has a business process improvement (reengineering) program been set up to lower costs, improve efficiencies and better support the customer (better-faster-cheaper)?

Step #9D—Attunement With People's Hearts and Minds

_____53. a. Do you have an HR Strategic (People) Plan in place?

_____54. b. Have all your people management/HR processes been assessed/audited and modified to support your Strategic Direction?

_____55. c. Do you have a specific identified list of each dysfunctional value and barrier to cultural change, along with a game plan to attack each one?

Step #10—Annual Strategic Review

_____56. Is the month/dates/sequence of the next Annual Strategic Review (and Update) set?

ebewc10.pmd

1420 Monitor Road • San Diego • California • 92110-1545 • (619) 275-6528 • Fax (619) 275-0324

SUMMARY: ENTERPRISE-WIDE EXECUTION

"The Devil's in the Details"

Explicit Tasks	Emphasis in Last Two Years	Need for Improvement	Comments
Steps #1-5: Strategic Planning			
Step #6: Business Unit Planning			
Step #7: Annual Action Priorities			
Step #7A: Annual Department Plans/Budgets			
Step #8: Smart Start Day			
Step #8A: Enterprise-Wide Change Skills			
Step #8B: Executive Development/ Accountability			
Step #8C: Project Teams			
Step #8D: Eliminate Bureaucracy/Fund the Change Process			
Step #8E: Change Agent Cadre Skills			
Step #8F: HR Best Practices			
Step #8G: Teams and Teamwork			
Step #9: Change Management Process (Rollercoaster)			
Step #9A: Change Management Structures in place			
Step #9B: Succession Planning			
Step #9C: Waves/Cascade of Change			
Step #10: Annual Strategic Enterprise-Wide Change Review			

ebewc10.pmd

1420 Monitor Road • San Diego • California • 92110-1545 • (619) 275-6528 • Fax (619) 275-0324

FIVE GUARANTEES OF SUCCESSFUL ENTERPRISE-WIDE CHANGE

1. Form a **Change Leadership Team** and have it meet for a full day every month with our standard agenda.

2. Set up an overall **Program Management Office** and an internal/external change management team with a support cadre of subject matter experts/facilitators.

3. Have **Project/Process Teams** for each Core Strategy and Key Initiative.

4. Set up a **"Yearly Comprehensive Map"** of the change process and fund it properly.

5. Have all department heads develop **Annual Department Plans** under the framework of your Core Strategies and top annual priorities.

Four Key Management Paradigms That Need Changing

1. From analytic to systems thinking

2. From conflict is bad to conflict is good

3. From self-protection to self-development (i.e., saving face)

4. From hierarchal change to Enterprise-Wide Change management

*These are the keys to success
in Enterprise-Wide Change*

Genius is
1% Inspiration
and
99% Perspiration

—Thomas A. Edison

---

ebewc10.pmd

1420 Monitor Road • San Diego • California • 92110-1545 • (619) 275-6528 • Fax (619) 275-0324

12 ABSOLUTES FOR SUCCESS IN ENTERPRISE-WIDE CHANGE

Create A Yearly Strategic Management Cycle – (Corporate-Wide Core Competency #3)

1. **Have a clear vision and positioning with shared values**—of your Ideal Future in the marketplace.

2. **Develop focused and shared core strategies**—as the *glue* for setting and reviewing annual goal setting and action planning for all major departments/SBUs, with a single page "tri-fold" to communicate the Enterprise-Wide Game Plan.

3. **Set up Quadruple Bottom Line Measures and a Tracking System**—to ensure clarity of purpose and focus on the scoreboard for success. Cascade it down in a Line-of-Sight for accountability of results at all levels – Unit-by-Unit/Dept.-by-Dept.

4. **Focus on the vital few leverage points of Business Excellence based on an Enterprise-Wide assessment of an Organization as a System. Create a Strategic Business Design with Watertight Integrity – Corporate-Wide Core Competency #3.**

5. **Set the Top Enterprise-Wide Change Priorities**—on only 2 pages to focus everyone on what's important next year.

6. **Conduct Large Group Enterprise-Wide Change Review and Critique Meetings**—to ensure that everyone knows and is "in sync" with everyone else.

7. **Institutionalize the Parallel Involvement Process**—with all key stakeholders as the new *participative* way you plan, change, and run your business day-to-day. Create a critical mass for Enterprise-Wide Change—that "goes ballistic" and becomes self-sustaining.

8. **Develop and gain public commitments of "Personal Leadership Plans (PLPs)": Develop & Achieve Leadership Excellence – Corporate-Wide Core Competency #1 —** by building a Leadership Development System for all supervisory and management leaders to achieve Leadership Excellence.

9. **Redo your HR Management Practices**—to support the positioning and values, especially your high performance management and Rewards system.

continued

continued

ebewc10.pmd

1420 Monitor Road • San Diego • California • 92110-1545 • (619) 275-6528 • Fax (619) 275-0324

12 ABSOLUTES FOR SUCCESS IN ENTERPRISE-WIDE CHANGE

10. **Establish an Enterprise-Wide Change Leadership Team**—led by the CEO and facilitated by a master external facilitator—with a single page, yearly comprehensive map of implementation—that meets on a monthly basis to lead all major changes.

11. **Set up a Program Management Office with "Strategic Sponsorship and/or Change Project Teams"** —of cross-functional leaders to develop, track, and monitor each core strategy. Use innovative Project/Progress Teams as the vehicle for change. Set up an "internal cadre" support team to support the Program Management Office.

12. **Conduct the Annual Enterprise-Wide Review (and Update)**—like an independent financial audit to ensure constant updating of your Enterprise-Wide Game Plan. This process begins to institutionalize **Corporate-Wide Core Competency #2 — "Build an Integrated, Yearly Strategic Management Cycle."**

STRATEGIC MANAGEMENT SYSTEM:
IT'S SIMPLE: ENTERPRISE-WIDE CHANGE

(Once You Use The Systems Thinking Approach™)

The Three Foundational Core Competencies of Every Organization on Earth:

1. Have a Shared Direction

A. Develop a Strategic Plan that is Customer-Focused
- with a shared Vision, Values and Core Strategies, pointing to a clear Future Positioning
- develop focused, organization-wide Action Priorities for the next year

B. Develop Buy-in and Stay-in to the Yearly Strategic Management Cycle and Plan
- communicate – communicate – communicate (stump speeches)
- involvement – participative management – and WIFFM

> **Core Competency #2: *Build an Integrated Strategic Management System***
> *– "Use Systems Thinking – Focus on the Customer"*

2. Develop and Implement Enterprise-Wide Change

A. Conduct a Strategic Business Assessment and Redesign
- to ensure the fit of all policies and parts, people and business processes of the organization – use *Building on the Baldrige*, a Fast Track Best Practices Assessment
- using the overall direction, Strategic Plan and positioning as the criteria

B. Conduct an Enterprise-Wide Change Process to Cascade down department work plans, budgets and accountability with Watertight Integrity and Accountability to the Shared Direction (level/level – unit/unit)
- using the core strategies, action priorities, and values as the glue to make Organization-Wide change down and throughout the organization

> **Core Competency #3: *Create a Strategic Business Design with Watertight Integrity –***
> *"Systematic problems require system-wide solutions."*

3. Develop Leaders Who Can Successfully Lead and implement Changes in the Shared Direction and Strategic Business Design

A. Know your role(s) as a leader

- **leaders**: focus on content and consequences
- **support cadre**: focus on processes and infra-structure coordination

B. Build follow-up structures and processes

- to track, adjust and achieve the plan and key success measures/results
- to reward, recognize and celebrate progress and results

> **Core Competency #1: *Develop and Achieve Leadership Excellence* –**
> *"Continually increase your range and depth of leadership skills through Leading Strategic Change and Innovation."*

ebewc10.pmd

1420 Monitor Road • San Diego • California • 92110-1545 • (619) 275-6528 • Fax (619) 275-0324

ENTERPRISE-WIDE CHANGE GAME PLAN TEMPLATE

Based on the Iceberg Theory of Change Framework

CONTENT OF THE CHANGE:

1. **Enterprise-Wide Change (EWC) Vision:** (including both economic alignment and cultural attunement issues)

2. **Any Missing Elements from your Clarity of Purpose?**
   (covered in Chapter Four, regarding E, A and B Phases of the Simplicity of Systems Thinking)

INFRASTRUCTURES FOR THE CHANGE:

3. **Main EWC Infrastructures:** (including the Program Management Office, Change Consultants and the Support Cadre plus the Change Leadership Team)

4. **EWC Substructures:** (such as an Employee Development Board, Rewards Team, Innovative Process/Project Teams, Technology Steering Committee, etc.)

5. **Clear Roles for the Players of Change:** (All four Roles plus Personal Leadership Plans for all executives, and the Parallel Involvement Process with all employees)

PROCESSES OF CHANGE:

6. **Leading, Managing and Re-creating the Change Processes:** (Including the Rollercoaster of Change's Six Stages, the Waves and waves of change, and the HR/People processes to support them)

EWC COMPETENCIES, COMMITMENT AND RESOURCES:

7. **Change Competencies:** (For executives, Change Consultants and all employees, including Systems Thinking)

8. **Commitment to the Perseverance Required:** (by the CEO, senior management, the Board of Directors and Change Consultant Cadre)

9. **EWC Resources:** (All types of resources needed are committed to and funded)

EWC YEARLY MAP OF IMPLEMENTATION:

10. **The detailed Map:** (including all Change Leadership Team meetings, the EWC Annual Strategic Review (and Update) and an EWC Capacity Review

ebewc10.pmd

1420 Monitor Road • San Diego • California • 92110-1545 • (619) 275-6528 • Fax (619) 275-0324

HOW TO GET STARTED

SEVEN DIFFERENT OPTIONS — TAILORED TO YOUR NEEDS

#1. Conduct a Strategic Planning Executive Briefing and Plan-to-Plan Day (or just ½ day briefing). From this tailor Strategic Planning to your needs.
- comprehensive Strategic Planning
- 3-year Business Planning
- Strategic Planning Quick
- Micro Strategic Planning

#2. Conduct a Enterprise-Wide Change Executive Briefing and Plan-to-Implement Day (or just ½ day briefing).

#3. Start at Any Point in the Cycle (Smart Start)
- Set up an Enterprise-Wide Change Leadership Team to guide and coordinate existing (in-process) change.
- Conduct annual planning via Core Strategy/Goals with top three action priorities for each.
- Finish budgeting and then set up Strategic Change Project Teams on big, cross-functional issues.
- Have an Annual Strategic Review (and Update) conducted as a starting point. Then proceed based on the recommendations/decisions from this audit.
- Have a "Strategic Business Design" assessment process/study conducted with recommendations on what to change. (Business Excellence Architecture)

#4. Conduct Training as a Way to Start (Build Your Capacity)
- Have internal staff get trained and licensed on strategic planning/facilitation.
- Have internal staff get trained and licensed on mastering strategic change and on *GoInnovate!*.
- Conduct a Visionary Leadership Practices Workshop to "kick-start" strategic planning.
- Conduct a Mastering Strategic Change Workshop simulation to "kick-start" or re-energize a major change project.
- Have your management trained in Strategic Planning concepts through a 2 or 3 day workshop on Strategic Planning ("Reinvented Strategic Management").

#5. Conduct Only What You Need Now
- Conduct a pilot strategic planning process for a Major Support Department or an Strategic Business Unit. Use it to learn and to develop internal cadre.
- Conduct only the Strategic Planning phase you need now—such as Visioning, measurements (Key Success Measures) or Core Strategy (issues) development . . . and then put in a Strategic Change Leadership Team to guide implementation.
- Have your management conference keynoted with a Strategic Planning/Strategic Change, 1-2 hour topic, using the 4-color models and 8-page summary articles as handouts.

#6. Conduct a major change on only 1-2 major change topics selected.

#7. Conduct Multi-Year "Drip-Drip" Joint Developmental Experiences (See next page)

ebewc10.pmd

1420 Monitor Road • San Diego • California • 92110-1545 • (619) 275-6528 • Fax (619) 275-0324

A STRATEGIC MANAGEMENT SYSTEM

(is the #2 Core Competency of Every Organization)

Time Management and Organization Effectiveness

A Systems Thinking Approach™ & Commitment

to a

Strategic Management System, and Cycle
(Planning, Leadership and Change)

is the **ultimate**

- Time Management
- Team Building
- Conflict Resolution
- Organizational Effectiveness and
- Executive Development tool

for

an entire organization.

THE RESULT: Business Excellence and Superior Results!

There is nothing else even close!
(All the rest are a series of well-meaning, piecemeal efforts)

ebewc10.pmd

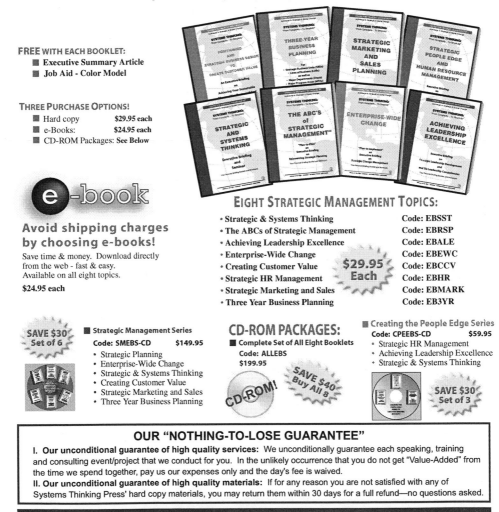

EXECUTIVE BRIEFING DAY
for Executives and Senior Management

Centre for Strategic Management®
Architects of Strategic Change

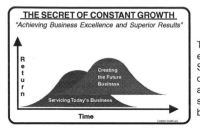

THE SECRET OF CONSTANT GROWTH
"Achieving Business Excellence and Superior Results"

ENHANCE YOUR "STRATEGIC IQ"™!

The Centre's Executive Briefing and Plan-To-Plan is designed to establish a common set of principles and knowledge on the specific Strategic Management project that your organization needs to develop or improve. By using this Systems Thinking Approach™ and principles, you can develop an Enterprise-Wide Game Plan for successful execution. Build your capacity to achieve and sustain business excellence and superior results.

Achieve Organizational Clarity, Simplicity and Superior Results!

EXECUTIVE BRIEFING DAY OUTLINE

AM - Executive Briefing : *"Educating and Assessing"*
- Choose from eight Strategic Managment Topics
- Learn the research on Proven Best Practices
- Assess your organization vs. these Best Practices Management Topics

PM - Plan-To-Plan Tasks: *"Organizing and Tailoring"*
- Organize and engineer success up front
- Tailor the change process to your needs
- Build a practical and realistic "Game Plan"

EIGHT EXECUTIVE BRIEFING DAY TOPICS
Strategic Management: The Systems Thinking Approach™

1. Strategic and Systems Thinking
2. Reinventing Strategic Planning
3. Enterprise-Wide Change
4. Creating the People Edge (Strategic HR Management)

5. Achieving Leadership Excellence
6. Becoming Customer Focused
7. Aligning Delivery & Distribution (Business Planning)
8. Creating Customer Value (Positioning & Design)

Science-Based Proven Research
- We are Interpreters and Translators of Proven Best Practices Research from the *Science of Living Systems*.
- We tailor these Best Practices into powerful, practical and easy to use, simple tools.

THE SYTEMS THINKING APPROACH™
- We own Systems Thinking Press™ the "Premier Publisher and Clearinghouse for Systems Thinking Resources".
- Visit our web site www.SystemsThinkingPress.com
- Learn about ALL our Strategic Management Materials.

NO FURTHER OBLIGATIONS
- There are NO Further Obligations after this day.
- WE will work with you ONLY if we are convinced you are seriously committed to success (why waste time & money)
- Success requires your understanding, discipline, persistence and leadership!

"Failing to Plan is Planning to Fail"   www.csmintl.com

**Systems
Thinking
Press™**

Specialists in Systems Resources
www.SystemsThinkingPress.com

Ordering Information

Send Order Form to: Systems Thinking Press - 1420 Monitor Road - San Diego, CA 92110-1545

Phone: 619-275-6528 - **Fax:** 619-275-0324 - **Email:** info@SystemsThinkingPress.com - **Website:** www.SystesmsThinkingPress.com

Date	_____			If rush order, need products by	_____
Name	_____			Title	_____
Company	_____				
Shipping Address	_____				

| City | _____ | State | _____ | Postal Code | _____ | Country | _____ |
| Phone | _____ | Fax | _____ | Email | _____ |

Quantity	Code	Description	Regular Price	Amount
	EBEWC	Executive Briefing - Leading Enterprise-Wide Change	call for rates	
			Sub Total	
			Sales Tax (CA residents only)	
			Shipping/handling charges	
			TOTAL (payable in US $)	

Payment Method ~ Please Check One

		Visa	Master Card	America Express	Discover
Credit Cards (processed in US Dollars)					
Credit Card #			Expiration Date		
Name on Card			Signature		
Check or Money Order Enclosed		Purchase Order (only for over $100)	PO#		

Shipping: Please choose a shipping method below. We make every attempt to ship the cheapest and best method. If you wish to be contacted with the shipping cost prior to your order being shipped, please check here

United States	**International**		
UPS Ground – 1 ½ weeks/less	Federal Express	International – One week or less	Priority International* – 2-3 days
UPS Three Day (business days)	UPS	International – One week or less	International Expedited* - 2-3 days
UPS Two Day (business days)	US Mail	Global Priority* - 1 ½ weeks or less	Global Express* - One week or less
UPS Next Day (business days)		*Not available in all areas.*	
US Postal Service			

Return Policy

You may return the products within 30 days of receipt for a refund (eProducts are not refundable). Shipping charges will not be refunded. A 20% (or greater) fee may be applied for items returned damaged. To assure proper credit, you must do three things: 1) return materials by a traceable means, 2) include a copy of your invoice, and 3) provide a reason for the return.

Our "Nothing-To-Loose Guarantee"

Our unconditional guarantee of high quality materials: if for any reason you are not satisfied with any of Haines Centre Assessments' materials, you may return them within 30 days for a refund – no questions asked.

We reserve the right to change prices without prior notice.

Systems Thinking Press
1420 Monitor Road · San Diego · CA · 92110-1545 · (619) 275-6528 · Fax (619) 275-0324
www.SystemsThinkingPress.com · Email info@SystemsThinkingPress.com

ebewc10.pmd

1420 Monitor Road • San Diego • California • 92110-1545 • (619) 275-6528 • Fax (619) 275-0324